A BARBARIAN

IN ASIA

'Govern the empire as you would cook a little fish.'

LAO-TSU

A BARBARIAN IN ASIA

★

HENRI MICHAUX

★

English Translation by Sylvia Beach

NEW DIRECTIONS

Manufactured in the United States of America
First published by New Directions in 1949
First published as New Directions Paperbook 622 in 1986
Published simultaneously in Canada
by Penguin Books Canada Limited

Library of Congress Cataloging-in-Publication Data

Michaux, Henri, 1899-1984
    A barbarian in Asia.
    (A New Directions Book)
    (New Directions paperbook; 622)
    1. Asia—Description and travel.   2. East Asia—
Description and travel.   3. National characteristics.
4. Michaux, Henri, 1899-1984—Journeys—Asia.
I. Title.
DS9.M443   1986   915'.04424   86-5362
ISBN 0-8112-0991-1 (pbk.)

Publisher's Note: Henri Michaux's *Un Barbare en Asie* was written in
the 1930s and first published in 1945. Over the years, Michaux's opinions
about some of the places he visited (in particular Japan) changed, and he
made some revisions in the French text. This New Directions Paperbook
edition of *A Barbarian in Asia*, however, is a reissue of the classic 1949
Sylvia Beach translation of the original version.

New Directions Books are published for James Laughlin
by New Directions Publishing Corporation,
80 Eighth Avenue, New York 10011

PREFACE FOR THE AMERICAN EDITION
OF 'A BARBARIAN IN ASIA'

As the most innocent mother knows, a baby is a dangerous propagandist who cries at the first opportunity and, in a tendencious and violent manner, creates a situation in which the people around him are not going to get the best of it.

People are not always *a priori* on the baby's side when they are not obliged to look after him.

Babies and writers know this and cleverly make use of it according to the strength of their voices, and the extent to which they are aware of their surroundings.

When I went on a journey to Asia twenty years ago, I was innocent enough to believe that I could give my impressions, and perhaps above everything I exulted in the great multiform, living challenge of the Asiatic peoples to our terrible Western monotony. Long live the last resistants!

As well as exulting, I certainly made propaganda, after my own fashion, for an endless variety of civilizations. (Down with the idea of only one!) There have been decades and decades of them. There could be, there can be more and more of them. Just as each child must make up his own personality out of a thousand different elements and a few chromosomes of various types, so the masses of men must make up a personality that will be called their civilization. A miners' union calls a strike—good. But suppose that instead they were to declare a miners' civilization. How strange it would be. What a lot we should have to learn from them. Wouldn't they shake us. And then we could have a South Pole civilization. Why not a Tennessee Valley civilization too?

When one reflects that the Papuans had their Papuan civilization, and complete and complex it was, one ought to feel hopeful.

Or must we be content forever with the economic sciences?

The most urgently needed science is one that will *show us how to make civilizations.*

Man needs a vast far-sighted aim, extending beyond his lifetime. A training rather than a hindrance for the coming planetary civilization.

To avoid war—construct peace.

HENRI MICHAUX

A BARBARIAN
IN INDIA

In India there is nothing to
see—everything to interpret.

Kabir was a hundred and twenty
years old and was going to die
when he sang:

I am drunk with joy
with the joy of youth
the thirty millions gods are there
I am going there—Happiness! Hap-
piness
I cross over the sacred circle . . .

I know some twenty capitals. Bah!

But then there is Calcutta. Calcutta, the most crowded city
in the Universe.

Imagine a city exclusively composed of ecclesiastics. Seven
hundred thousand ecclesiastics (plus another 700,000 inhabitants indoors—the women. They are a head shorter than the
men and they never go out). One is only among men—an extraordinary sensation.

The Bengali is a born ecclesiastic, and ecclesiastics, with
the exception of the very small ones who are carried, always
go on foot.

Everyone is a pedestrian—on the pavement or in the middle of the street . . . tall and slender with no hips, no shoulders,
no gestures, no laughter.

The most varied costumes.

Some are almost naked; but a true ecclesiastic is always
an ecclesiastic. The most naked ones are perhaps the most
dignified. Some are dressed in togas with two folds thrown

3

back, or with one fold thrown back—mauve, pink, green, wine-colored togas—or in white robes. They are too numerous for the streets and for the city. All of them are self-assured, with a mirror-like expression, an insidious sincerity and the kind of impudence that come from meditating with the legs crossed.

The way they look at you is perfect, neither up nor down, without pride or apprehension.

When they are standing up their eyes might belong to a man lying down. Lying down, to a man standing up. Unwavering eyes, unbending and trapped.

An unself-conscious insolent crowd basking in itself, or rather each in himself, but a crowd that can be cowardly and stupid if attacked and taken by surprise.

Each individual is watched over by his seven centers, by his lotuses, his heavens, by his morning and evening prayers to Kali, with meditation and sacrifice.

Everyone intent on avoiding any kind of pollution such as laundrymen, leather workers, Mohammedan butchers, fishermen, cobblers or handkerchiefs which retain what belongs on the ground, the sickening breath of Europeans (with the odor of murdered victims clinging to it), and in general the innumerable causes for a man's being continually plunged up to his neck in mud, if he is not careful.

Always on guard (those who are born stupid become twice as stupid, and who is stupider than a stupid Hindu), slow, controlled and self-inflated. (In Indian plays and films, traitors who are unmasked and the Rajah's officer who draws his sword in rage never take action immediately. They require about thirty seconds in which to 'color' their anger.)

Concentrated, abandoning themselves reluctantly to the rush and torrent of existence, self-contained, highly charged.

Never crushed, never at the end of their tether, never at a loss. Assured and impudent.

Sitting wherever they want to; when they get tired of carrying a basket, putting it on the ground and throwing themselves down alongside it; meeting a barber in the street, or at a crossroads and saying, 'Well, what if I did have a shave . . .' and getting shaved right then and there in the middle of the street, quite unperturbed by the traffic, sitting in any place except where one might expect to find them—on the road, in front of benches, amongst the goods on the shelves in their shops, beside hats or pairs of shoes, on the grass, in the hot sun (they feed on the sun), in the shade (they feed on the shade), or at the border line between sun and shade, conversing among the flowers in the parks, or just alongside a bench or AGAINST it (does one ever know where a cat is going to sit?). These are the ways of the Hindu. Oh, those devastated lawns in Calcutta. No Englishman can look at that grass without an inward shudder. But no police on earth, no battery of guns would prevent them from sitting wherever it suits them.

Motionless and not expecting anything from anyone.

Anyone who feels in the mood for singing, sings, for praying, prays aloud, while he sells his betel-nut or no matter what.

A city incredibly full of pedestrians, always pedestrians, so that one can hardly make one's way through even the widest streets.

A city of canons and of their master, their master in impudence and unconcern, the cow.

They have allied themselves with the cow, but the cow does not care. The cow and the monkey, the two most impudent of the sacred animals. There are cows all over Calcutta.

5

They cross the streets, stretch out at full length on the pavement which is thus rendered useless, deposit their dung in front of the Viceroy's car, inspect the shops, threaten the elevators, install themselves on your doorstep, and if the Hindu were good to nibble, no doubt he would be nibbled.

As for her indifference towards the outer world, herein again she is the Hindu's superior. Obviously she seeks neither explanation nor truth in the outer world. It is all *Maya*. This world is Maya. It does not matter. And when she eats nothing but a tuft of grass, she needs more than seven hours to meditate upon that.

So they abound, and they roam, and they meditate all over Calcutta; a race that does not mix with any other, like the Hindu, like the English, the three peoples inhabiting this capital of the World.

★

Never, never, will the Hindu realize to what a degree he exasperates the European. The spectacle of a Hindu crowd, of a Hindu village, or even crossing a street where the Hindus are in their doorways, is irritating and odious.

They are all constipated.

You cannot get used to it.

You always hope that by the next day they will have recovered.

This constipation is the most irritating of all, constipation of the breathing and of the soul.

They look at you with self-control, a mysterious locking-up, and though it is not clear, give the impression of interfering somewhere inside one, as it would be impossible for oneself to do.

★

The Hindu does not succumb to the charm of animals. Ah! No indeed. He rather looks askance at them.

He dislikes dogs. No concentration, dogs. Creatures of impulse, shamefully lacking in self-control.

And in the first place, what are all these reincarnations doing here? If they had not sinned they would not be dogs. Perhaps they were loathsome criminals, perhaps they killed a Brahmin (in India one must avoid being either a dog or a widow).

The Hindu appreciates wisdom and meditation. He is in harmony with the cow and the elephant, who keep things to themselves and live in retirement as it were. The Hindu likes animals that do not say 'thank you' and that do not turn too many somersaults.

In the country there are peacocks, no sparrows, but peacocks, ibises, herons, an enormous number of crows and some kites.

All that is serious.

Some camels and some water buffalos.

Needless to say, the water buffalo is slow. The water buffalo wants to lie in the mud. Outside of that, he is not interested. And when harnessed, even in Calcutta, he will not go fast, oh! no, and from time to time, passing his soot-coloured tongue between his teeth, he will gaze at the city like one who feels he has gone astray.

As for the camel, he is quite the superior of the horse, orientally speaking; a trotting or a galloping horse always looks as if he were going in for a sport, he does not run, he struggles. The camel, on the contrary, carries himself rapidly forward with a harmonious gait.

7

Now that we are on the subject of cows and elephants, there is something I want to say. Lawyers are not to my taste. Cows and elephants, beasts who lack the vital impulse, and lawyers.

And regarding impulse, I want to say something. The first time I went to the Hindustani theater, I nearly cried with rage and disappointment. I was right out in 'the provinces.'

An avalanche of despicable and ridiculous words.

Hindustani is a language containing eight or nine languages. But all the words have the same look:

Gaping in a broad, good-natured peasant fashion, slow, with an enormous number of very thick vowels, â's and ô's with a sort of buzzing, heavy vibration, or a dragging, disgusted contemplativeness, î's and particularly ê's, a fool's letter, a real cow's bê. All this, enveloped, sickening, comfortable, eunuch-like, satisfied, devoid of a sense of the ridiculous.

Bengali is more singing, a slope, the tone one of gentle remonstrance, of good humour and suavity, the vowels succulent and a sort of incense.

★

The white man possesses a quality that has enabled him to make his way: *disrespect.*

Disrespect being empty-handed must fabricate.

The Hindu is *religious,* he feels that he is connected with everything.

The American has hardly anything. And even that is too much. The white man does not allow himself to be hypnotized by anything. If you are absorbed by studies, games, sports or family you are not modern.

8

In former times the learned men of India and everywhere were lost in wonder at the phenomena that were to be observed, by chance, right in front of their eyes. They looked no further but brought to these their labor of comparison and of syllogism. Anyhow, it helped to pass the time. Three thousand years, for example.

Arabs, Hindus, even the lowest of the Pariahs seem to be possessed with the idea of the *nobility* of man. Their gait, their robe, their turban, their way of dressing. And the Europeans here all look like plain workmen or errand-boys.

★

All Hindu thought is magic.

A thought must be active, act directly on the inner being, on the outer being.

The formulae of Western science do not act directly. No formula acts directly on the wheelbarrow, not even the formula of levers. One is obliged to put one's hands to it.

Western philosophies make one's hair fall out and shorten one's life.

Oriental philosophy makes hair grow and prolongs life.

A great deal of what passes for fine philosophic-religious thought is nothing at all but *Mantras* or magic prayers, with a property much the same as 'Open, Sesame!'

If these words (to quote from the *Kandogya-Upanishad* concerning a text which, in spite of all the commentaries, does not appear to be so extraordinary) *were said to an old stick, it would be covered with flowers and leaves and would take root again.*

One must not forget that all the hymns and often mere

9

philosophical commentaries are *efficacious*. They are not thoughts to think, they are thoughts for the participation in Being, in BRAHMA.

And the Hindu, ever scrupulous, displays a special concern with the matter.

To be detached from the Absolute, that hell to which you Europeans are going, that hell haunts them.

Beware of this frightful place!

'For those who leave this world without having discovered the Atman and his true life, there will be no liberty in ANY WORLD' (VIII, Prapâthaka Khonda 2 *Kh. Upanishad*).

One cannot think of that without feeling frozen.

Most of the Hindus I have known, employed by English firms, possessed one or two good 'formulae.'

And the Indian armies always used as a weapon of combat the magic formulae of the *Mantras*.

★

Controlled breathing for magic purposes may be considered the national Hindu exercise.

One day, at the station in Seranpore, I asked a *babu* who was accompanying me to explain one of the details of this subject.

In less than three minutes, about twenty experimentalists, advisers, propagators were around us, attracted by this miraculous science, and with the aid of the nose (four inhalations with the left nostril, hold it, then sixteen rapid exhalations with the right, etc., etc. . . .), were spreading before us the crumbs of their extraordinary science of respiration.

Never did I see so many gestures (the Hindu lives without gestures).

10

More than one clerk in the Imperial Bank, when his work is done, occupies himself with *Mantras;* he has his *guru* and dreams of retiring to the bastions of the Himalayas for meditation.

★

In the deep sense of the word, the Hindu is practical. From the realm of the spirit he expects returns. Beauty he does not value. Beauty is an intermediary. Truth, as such, he does not value—only the Efficacious. That is why his promoters are successful in America, and make proselytes in Boston and in Chicago, where he is side-by-side with . . . Pelman.

★

I had lost all hope of finding out what idolatry was about. Now, at least, I have seen one kind of it. The Hindu is steeped in idolatry. Anything will do, but he must have his idol. He 'joins' the idol. He draws its power from it. He must idolize.

The *Rig Veda* is full of hymns to the elements, to Agni the fire, to the Air, to Indra the heavens, and to the sun.

They always adore it.

In the morning, they precipitate themselves from trains to come and salute it (and I am not confusing them with Mohammedans).

If they happen to be performing their ablutions in the Ganges when the sun rises, they salute it with devotion.

The Hindu has a thousand idols.

Does Don Juan love women? Hum. He loves to love. The Hindu adores to adore. He cannot help it.

Love is not what they feel for Gandhi; they adore him,

11

his portrait is in all the temples, it is prayed to. Through him they communicate with God.

The Hindu adores his mother, the maternity of his mother, the potential maternity of little girls, the infancy of the child.

He possesses five sacred trees.

When the wife of the head schoolmaster in a village near Shandernagor died, her footprints were taken, these prints were reproduced in red in the temple, beside the statue of a god, and each of the pupils adored 'the mother.'

The Hindu likes to bow down.

The cult of Vivekananda, who died not so very long ago (and who had, they assured me, succeeded in attaining divinity, by the Mohammedan, Christian, Buddhist method, etc.), is carefully kept up. His breakfast is brought at eight o'clock to the room that he occupied at the end of his life, at Belur, at noon another meal, at one o'clock, the moment when he was accustomed to rest, his photograph is laid on the bed and covered with a sheet. In the evening his photograph is brought downstairs so that he may say his prayer to Kali.

The Hindu wants to give worship, therefore he prefers to see the maternal rather than the feminine in woman, but naturally he takes care to maintain communication with everything. The Being swarms on every side, nothing should be overlooked, and as he is exceedingly sensual, he knows quite well, besides, how to place himself in communication with universal fornication.

It was not many years ago that the great ascetic Ramakrishna wore women's dress so that he might feel himself to be the mistress of Krishna, the God who lived among men.

★

There is something incomparably splendid in this whole Hindu people, that always seeks the most and not the least, that has been the foremost to deny the visible world, for which, not only spiritually, but physically, it does not care, the people of the Absolute, a radically religious people.

The Christian religious sentiment (though they have got Jesus Christ just where they want him, and often speak of him as 'one of themselves,' an Asiatic, etc.) has a different aspect from the Hindu religious sentiment.

Lord, Lord, from the lowest depths, I cried unto thee.

'De profundis clamavi ad te, Domine.' Here are words that release a fundamental Christian feeling, humility.

When you enter the cathedral at Cologne, no sooner inside and you are at the bottom of the ocean and only above, high above, is the gate of life . . . : 'De profundis,' you enter and you are immediately lost. You are nothing now but a mouse. Humility, 'praying Gothic.'

The Gothic cathedral is built in such a way that he who enters it is overcome by weakness.

And you pray there on your knees, not on the ground, but on the edge of a chair, the centers of natural magic dispersed. Unfortunate and inharmonious position in which you can only sigh, and try to tear yourself away from your misery: 'Kyrie Eleison, Kyrie Eleison,' Lord, have mercy.

The Hindu religions* on the contrary do not bring out the weakness of man, but his strength. Prayer and meditation are the exercise of spiritual *forces*. Beside Kali one may see the table demonstrating the *attitudes* of prayer. He who prays well makes stones fall, perfumes the waters. A prayer is a rape. Good tactics are required.

* *Buddhism excepted, but long ago Buddhism abandoned India. Too pure for them.*

13

The interior of temples (even those that on the outside are the largest) is tiny, tiny, in order that one may be aware of one's strength. There will be twenty niches, rather than one grand altar. The Hindu must be aware of *his strength*.

So he says AUM. Serenity and power. Magic at the center of all magic. One should hear them sing it in the *Vedic Hymns,* the *Upanishads* or the *Tantra of the great liberation.*

Joy in mastery, taking possession, the assured raid on the divine body. With one of them, I remember, there was a sort of cupidity, of spiritual ferocity that spat, victorious in the face of misfortune and of the lower demons. With others a positive bliss, limited and classified, one that could never be taken away from them again.

The uniting of the individual mind with God. This kind of seeking is by no means rare. A great many Hindus are entirely occupied with it. It is not at all exceptional. But to succeed is another thing.

Towards half past six in the evening at sundown, you hear over the whole countryside and in the villages the very loud sound of the conch-shells. This is a sign that the people are praying (excepting the lowest of wretches, each one in his pagoda, of stone, of wood or of bamboo covered with leaves). They pray and soon roll on the ground possessed by the Goddess Kali or any other. These faithful are well-meaning people who have been taught such-and-such a practice and who, like most of those who go in for religion, flounder about when they reach a certain level and never get any further.

Well-meaning people, one never does know whether to laugh or to cry. One of them whom I had seen thus engaged (though they are careful, as a rule, to avoid praying in the presence of Europeans) said to me: 'Today I have only attained a small part of God.'

Even Hindu ecstasy in its highest forms must not be confused with the mysterious ways of the Christian mystic. *Saint Angela of Foligno, Saint Francis of Assisi, Saint Lydwine of Schiedam* attained it by self-laceration, the *Admirable Ruysbroek, Saint Joseph of Cupertino,* by frightful humility, so by dint of being nothing and entirely stripped, they were snapped up by the Divinity.

★

Nothing is sadder than failure. Rarely do the religious Hindus bear the mark of divinity. They have it as the critic of the *'Times'* and professors of literature in schools have the stamp of literary genius.

Faith with them as with us is extremely significant.

At the door of temples one often sees two rows of beggars provided with touching appeals to faith. They are like large carved wooden figures: a man lies stretched on the ground—this man is dead—a woman on her knees is gazing in astonishment.

This woman has the promise of a God (is it Siva? I cannot recollect) that she will bear a hundred children. A hundred—and her husband is dead, there he is, and he has only given her so far eighteen children. Moreover, widows do not remarry.

'Huh! promising me a hundred children.' Then she waits for the God to show what he can do, and Siva (but it can't be Siva) is touched, and forced by her faith, resuscitates the husband.

What I am telling here is the story according to the expression of the group. But the Hindus do not know how to paint, still less how to carve a natural expression. That is why I am inclined to think that the woman's attitude should be a little more respectful.*

★

One has not been sufficiently struck by the slowness of the Hindu mind. Especially the Bengali mind, which is like a caricature of it.

It is essentially slow, under control.

His sentences, when one hears them spoken, sound as if they were being spelled. His songs also. His music is a music that takes its time.

The Hindu does not run in the street, nor do his thoughts run in his brain. He walks. He moves step by step.

The Hindu does not rush. He is never elliptic. He does not stand out from the group. He is the exact opposite of the climax. He never bowls you over. In the 125,000 verses of the *Ramayanas,* in the 250,000 of the *Mahabharata* there is not a flash.

The Hindu is not in a hurry. He reasons with his feelings.

He likes things to be linked up together.

Sanscrit is the most interlinked language in the world, undoubtedly the finest creation of the Hindu mind. A panoramic language, a language for logicians, flexible, sensitive and attentive, a language of foresight, swarming with cases and declensions.

The Hindu is abundant, and he has this abundance well

A man, to them, has not two arms. He has eight, he has sixteen, he has twenty, he is pierced all over with arms.

What postcards do they sell in India? Nothing but postcards representing man from a magic viewpoint. Luminous circumferences on the forehead, at the navel, at the sexual organ . . ., flowers, forces, here is THEIR MAN.

16

in hand, liking sweeping views, and seeing them quite well too.

Drona has just died. His father is informed of it.

Unhurried, the father, in 240 quite slow, quite circumstantial, quite regular sentences, asks questions while no one can get in a word.

After that he faints. He is fanned. He awakes. And he goes at it again. A new lot of from 200 to 250 questions.

Then a halt.

Now, equally unhurriedly, and beginning with an account of the flood, a bystander gives his version of the affair.

About an hour and a half is spent in this way.

As there are several wars at home and abroad in the *Mahabharata,* with several interventions on the part of the gods and heroes, one can easily see why its 250,000 verses are barely sufficient to give an idea of this affair.

His thought is a projectile, its speed always the same.

Needless to say, the center of the *Mahabharata* is not easy to find. And the epic note is never abandoned an instant. The *epic* note, in fact, like the *erotic* note has something naturally false, artificial and forced about it, and appears to be made for the straight line.

When you have compared a brave soldier to a tiger among rabbits, and to a herd of elephants in front of a young bamboo, and to a hurricane carrying ships away, you can continue on like that for ten hours but you won't get us to raise our heads again. You reached the summit immediately and you go straight ahead.

The erotic works likewise. After two or three rapes, a few flagellations and acts against nature, say what you may, the astonishment wears off, and you fall asleep over your book.

That is because one is not by nature either epic or erotic.

17

Often I have been struck by the facility with which the Hindus *take* the *'sursum corda'* note, and the note of the redemptionist preacher. This note is connected with their way of progressing, with their unilateral way of thought.

★

What is a thought? A phenomenon that betrays the making of a mind—its frame—and what this frame desires.

We ourselves feel and understand by dividing by two, three and four. The Hindu into sixty-four, thirty-two, rarely nine, almost always into numbers above twenty. He is extremely abundant. Never does he see a situation in three or four subdivisions.*

Gautama, though he has a contemplative mind, expresses his first illumination thus:

From ignorance come the *Sankharas*.

From the *Sankharas* comes consciousness.

From consciousness come name and form.

From name and form come the six provinces.

From the six provinces comes the contact.

From the contact comes feeling.

---

* *Needless to say, our division by two or three does not correspond more closely to reality. 'To be animate, to be inanimate, warm or cold, those who are seasick, those who are not seasick.' Though the physical and natural sciences have showed us, and we* KNOW *that it is not as simple as all that, we continue to divide by two, even when we are obliged to follow up our division by corollaries, and by restrictions such as 'yes but,' and 'there is also . . .'*

The Hindu foresees everything.

And if he does not possess the thirty-four elements for dividing a question, he will invent the ten or fifteen that he lacks.

Like the European who, though he knows nothing about an affair, nevertheless begins by dividing it into three.

From feeling comes thirst.

From thirst comes attachment.

From attachment comes existence.

From existence comes birth.

From birth comes old age, death, sorrow, lamentations, suffering, prostration, despair.

A little later (see Digha and Maghima Nahaya) he refutes the sixty-two primordial heresies concerning the Being.

Already a syllogism, or the linking together of three terms seems to me risky. I have no confidence in it. The Hindu, even when a visionary, requires at least nine, eleven, forty or more.

He is never simple, never natural, always applying himself.

When you see one of his thoughts in forty points, what does that prove? Well, it proves that the author is content, that he has succeeded in filling the frame of his mind.

Nor is it a refinement. A sharpening, anything sudden upsets the Hindu: he waits to see what comes next.

The whole, the chain, that is all that matters to him. The subject itself is of no consequence. Whether it has to do with books, religion or love treatises, you always have the twenty to thirty propositions partially linked up again. As though one were hearing scales, immense scales.

★

One must not forget that India happens to be in the Middle East, like Arabia, Persia, and Asiatic Turkey.

The land of pink, pink houses, *Saris* edged with pink, valises painted pink, liquid butter, sweetish, flavorless dishes, cold and sickening, and what is more insipid than the poet Kalidasa when he sets out to write insipid poetry?

The Arab, so violent with his language that is like belching, the Arab, hard and fanatic, the Turk, a conqueror and cruel, these are also peoples with nauseating perfumes, rose jam and loukoum.

Take a look at the Alcazar at Granada—you need go no further if you want to know this taste for titillating little pleasures that the Arabs have put into architecture, these irritating arabesques, neither inside nor outside the wall, strictly regulated, complicated and never letting themselves go; outdoors, a hermetic garden frosted with rare strips of greenery, and a small rectangle of water, flat and shallow, and a small spout like a thread, shooting high in the air, and falling with a noise that is petty, and at the same time secret and extenuated. And somehow, from the whole thing one gets the effect of a draught.

But one must see the Taj Mahal at Agra.

Beside it, Notre Dame of Paris is a block of garbage, good for pitching into the Seine, or dumping anywhere, like all, all the other monuments (excepting, perhaps, the Parthenon and a few wooden pagodas).

Take the following ingredients: white bread, milk, talcum powder and water; mix this and make with it an outrageous mausoleum; make a gaping, formidable gateway, big enough to admit a squadron of cavalry, but through which only a coffin entered. Do not forget the oh! so useless windows of marble trellis (for the material of which I speak and of which the edifice is built is an extremely delicate marble, exquisite—almost sickly—that is going to dissolve any minute, a rain will melt it this very evening, though it has been standing intact and virginal for three centuries, with its irritating, disturbing girlish structure). Do not forget the useless marble windows where the so deeply regretted one, the regretted one of the Grand Mogul, of Shâh Jehan may come to linger in the cool of the evening.

In spite of its strictly formal ornamentation, one that is purely geometrical, the Taj Mahal floats. The door gives onto a wave. In the cupola, the immense cupola, there is a trifle too much of something, a mere trifle that everyone is aware of, something that is painful. Everywhere the same unreality. For this whiteness is not real, it has no weight, is not solid. False in the sun. False in the moonlight, a kind of silver fish built by man in nervous excitement.

★

The Englishman washes himself with great regularity. Nevertheless, to the Hindu he is the symbol of defilement and uncleanliness. The Hindu can hardly think of him without vomiting.

This is because the Englishman is continually soiled by various contacts that the Hindu carefully avoids.

Few creatures bathe themselves as frequently as the Hindu.

At Chandernagor, which is smaller than Asnières, there are sixteen hundred ponds, plus the Ganges, whose waters are sacred. Well, you can pass by at any hour of the day, and you will rarely find one of them unoccupied. And the Ganges, of course, does not remain empty. The Ganges does not flow with distilled water, naturally. One takes it as it comes. The water in the ponds likewise. If this water were clean one would not dirty it on purpose before bathing oneself.

And in the water, the Hindu's behavior is serious. Very erect, the water up to his knees. From time to time he stoops down, and the sacred water of the Ganges passes over him, and he gets up. He spends some time in this manner; he also washes his *dhouti*.* He is particularly careful to wash his teeth. He establishes relations with the sun by prayer, if he sees it.

But no laughing. Near some of the great urban centers, however, in the vicinity of jute factories, you sometimes see, though rarely, a few rascals trying to do the 'crawl.' The 'crawl'! Swimming! swimming, in sacred water. One or two have even been seen to splash each other. These sights, happily, are rare, rare and without a sequel.

Yet, in spite of it all, Hindu dirt is proverbial.

Curiously enough, when their painters make pictures of their filthy interiors, of their people in rags, the pictures are perfectly clean. The dirt is indicated quite cleanly. The rents in the rags are clean, the spots are clean; which seems to imply that they lack nothing.

Whereas, when you look at European pictures of the nineteenth century, you only find coal merchants in them, leprous houses and walls, slimy faces, dirty interiors.

★

The Hindu is a reinforced being. He reinforces himself by means of meditation. He is high-pressured.

There is a difference between a European and a Hindu, a difference like that between silence and a note on an organ. The Hindu is always intense, his repose is positive. The white man's repose is zero, or ràther it is minus x.

The Hindu is a sensualist: he takes delight slowly.

The exceptional place that he occupies in the spiritual

* *A kind of tunic.*

22

world is due to the fact that he has always sought enjoyment in satisfying the most remarkable appetites.

In religion and in sacrifice, in adoration, in magic power and . . . in an extraordinary vanity.

The rajahs have trained thousands of Hindu menials for thousands of years to be cringing cowards.

And this cringing, inconceivable to one who has not seen it, is more frightful, more painful to behold than all the miseries and the famine and the endemic cholera.

This cringing of caste, the cringing born of three thousand years of male and female cringing, was made for their benefit. And look at the result.

Only princes and quite rich people use Royal Yakuti.

These are the headlines of a stupendous advertisement. For a patent medicine, and not such a tremendously high-priced one at that.

This advertisement with its appeal to the flashy has done more to sell the stuff than a hundred thousand medical certificates.

Without their vanity, the institution of caste would not have held out for three thousand years.

Christian converts have had a partition built in the cathedral at Pondicherry to separate the castes.

I am a Christian, but of the Brahmin caste!

When a creature that is nothing colors his nothingness, possibly it makes him happier, but he is twice nothing to others.

No one knows to what extent people of inferior caste can be stupid, absolutely stupid and impervious where intelligence, or rather presence of the spirit is concerned.

★

Most of them tall and slender, with no shoulders, no calves of the legs, no muscles, very feminine, the face often flat, with eyes like a toad, never taken off you and from which nothing is to be extracted. Hairdressers' dummies.

Not meditative, but sticky, or rather, stuck.

A brilliancy in their gaze such as beauty products give, which gives you pleasure to look at, but which you will not turn to see again.

Admirable black hair, very vivid, supple, long.

Some fine faces—those of well-born people (extremely rare).

Some old men, with magnificent heads, veritable fathers of humanity, ancestors of music and of wisdom, harmoniously developed.

Nowhere is there a sparkle.

Faces of amoral people who are content, and of false witnesses who are justified.

No humanity whatsoever.

The Hindu's mind is not actually on beauty. Beauty is not what matters. They can do without it. They have none in their homes. Neither in their houses nor elsewhere.

If they must have beauty, then it will be a superabundance, the lascivious, the rococo.*

But they prefer 'nothing at all.'

Their paintings and sculptures were, however, very beautiful, were beautiful almost in spite of themselves. The Hindu has the taste, the feeling and the vice for seduction, but also for the academic. The Hindu likes recipes, figures, strict symbols, grammar.

When I arrived in Colombo, and went into the museum,

* *I have read attentively the marriage of* RAMA *and of* SITA. *No doubt, it was brilliant, but oh! how pretentious it must have been.*

a celebrated one, mind you, I began after a while to run instead of walk through the rooms. I was in despair. Oh! Academy! Ah! the apes! Little do I care whether it be a first- or a second-class ape. When all of a sudden I saw something. In one of the fresco rooms. Awkwardness, impulsiveness, an excited groping, an eagerness to excel, an emotion that springs from daylight and from warm bodies executed in a style as yet ill-defined, the attitudes, all surprise and willingness—the frescos of Sigeriya (sixth century) (Buddha preaching at the Court of the Queen, etc.). So they too once had their inspiration, a warm and vital inspiration.

This did not happen often. Only the paintings of *Ajanta* gave me an impression of fellow-feeling. All of it being of the *Gupta* period, the age also of Kalidasa. It is well to remember that for eight centuries the Hindus have been under the foreigner's domination (Moslems, English).

The rest is academic stuff with which all immense rooms of the museums are filled, and where, naturally, a lot of old nodding archeologists, who have never written, nor engraved, nor carved anything artistic whatsoever, have laid down the law, and given Europeans the duty of admiring it.

Of all the railway stations in the world, the station at Calcutta is the most remarkable. All the others are eclipsed by it. Only this one is a station.

Not that the building itself is so extraordinary. No doubt it is. But before Calcutta I never fully realized what a station could be.

What is it? a place where people wait for trains.

In Calcutta they *really* do wait.

25

There are about twenty tracks and as many platforms.

The entrance to each platform is guarded by an iron gate.

Between these gates and the city of Calcutta is the immense hall of the station.

This hall is a dormitory. Every one of the travelers is to be found sleeping here. In front of the gate that separates them from the approaching train they lie, sleeping with one eye open on their pink valises.

This impression of the rails beyond, of the trains that presently are going to carry you away, this sleep is a preliminary, to make believe that sometimes you wait a week or two before laying eyes on your train. (Naturally, the waiting rooms are unoccupied. Too far from the train, too full of seats.) This waiting for departure—and yet this sleep.

These people, dead tired at the mere thought of traveling. Intent on getting their rest, above all, their rest.

This is a unique impression.

And there are always thousands of Hindus in this station, between whose bodies you have to pick your way, stepping warily as on swampy ground, and after a struggle reaching your compartment followed by a few eternal eyes.

All the 'best' people in India gave it up, from the beginning, gave up India and the whole earth.

The great miracle of the English is that now the Hindus do care about it.

★

If the Christians had wanted to convert the Hindus, instead of ten thousand 'average' missionaries, they would have sent one saint.

One saint alone would convert millions of Hindus.

No race is more responsive to holiness.

★

Chastity is the starting-point of magic.

The Hindus reproach the Catholic missionaries (who almost all observe their vows of chastity) for not profiting enough from it, for not deriving a spiritual strength directly from it. *What does this mean exactly?*

The Jesuit who put this question to me had the eyes of a small boy, of a schoolboy, not the eyes of a man.

I might have made use of the fact when replying, but I preferred to reflect upon it at leisure.

Some Hindus are still of the opinion that Europe should 'rest' on Asia. But Europe is unable to rest on anyone. It can rest no more. The time for resting is past. All we can do now is to see whether anything can be made with what is left.

Besides, resting did not produce enough.

★

Another difference between the Hindu's way of praying and the European's is this—an all-important difference: the Hindu prays naked, as naked as possible, covering only the chest or the belly if he is in delicate health.

This is no time to be proper. He prays alone in the dark under the motionless world.

There must be no intermediary, no clothing between the All and one's self, nor must one feel any division whatsoever of the body.

The Hindu is also perfectly happy to pray while bathing.

A Hindu who said, in my presence, his prayer to *Kali,* removed his clothing, except for a small belt, and told me: 'When I pray alone at sunset, and naked, I pray more easily.'

All clothing cuts one off from the world. Whereas, lying stretched in the dark, the All flows to you and carries you away in its wind.

While making love to his wife, the Hindu thinks of God, of whom she is an aspect and a particle.

How fine it must be to have a wife who understands this, who spreads immensity above the small and yet so disturbing and decisive love-shock, above this sudden, great abandonment.

This communion in the infinite, at such a moment of mutual pleasure, must be really an experience that enables you to look people in the eye afterward, with a magnetism that cannot retreat, holy and at the same time lustral, impudent and shameless; even the animals, say the Hindus, must communicate with God, so odious to them is limitation of any kind.*

There are even Hindus who masturbate while thinking of God. They say that it would be worse still to make love to a woman (European style)—she individualizes you too much, and does not know how to pass on from the idea of love to that of the All.

★

The Hindu is greedy: he holds a third of the world's money.

* *I have kept some postcards of the temple of Kornarak, and of its statues. The heads are beautiful, contemplative, lost in bliss.*
The bodies with enormous sexual organs are joined in various positions, and onanism is not excluded.

28

He thesaurizes. He likes to appraise his gold, his pearls. To think about his potentiality.

On a spiritual plane, he is greedy for God. One pictures the Hindus as leeches on God's surface.

Vivekananda to Ramakrishna. His first question: 'Have you seen God?'

Dhan Gopal, returning from America, inquires about his brother: 'Has he seen God?'

Have you *had God?* would be more nearly what they have in their minds.

The Yogi economizes his strength. This superman resembles the ox. Never reaches the painful, live center of himself, *willfully* avoids it. Sanscrit, a *possessive* language.

The Hindu's love of the Homeric explanation, the embracing, magnetic description, that *imposes* the vision.

To him, a horse, plain and simple, is no horse; you must tell him—horse with four legs, with four shoes, with a belly, a sexual organ, two ears; the horse must be carved inside of him.

Venerable Nagarena, what virtues must a disciple possess? (Question of King Milinda).

Reply:

1) one virtue of the ass
2) two of the cock
3) one of the squirrel
4) one of the she-panther
5) two of the he-panther
6) five of the tortoise
7) one of the bamboo
8) one of the goose
9) two of the crow
10) two of the monkey, etc.

29

34) two of the anchor, etc.

36) three of the pilot

37) one of the mast, etc.

61) two of the sowing, etc., etc.

There are sixty-seven divisions and more than a hundred virtues.

No wonder so many virtues are required, nor even that it takes three hundred pages to explain them, to describe minutely the ass with its two ears, the cock with its spurs . . . leaving nothing obscure, but it is astonishing that he *knows all this in advance*. That, however, is the Hindu mind—broad, panoramic, possessive, sensual. The opposite of the Chinaman, who is all allusions, detours and brief contacts.

When I saw the Turks on the one hand, and on the other the Armenians, without knowing anything about their history, I felt that in a Turk's skin I would beat up an Armenian with great pleasure, and as an Armenian I should have to be beaten up.

When I saw the Moroccans on the one hand, and on the other hand the Jews, I understood why the Moroccans always enjoyed violating the wives of the Jews right in front of their noses and always did so.

This can be explained. But then it turns out to be quite another thing.

The first time a snake sees a mongoose it feels that the encounter will be fatal to itself, a snake. As for the mongoose, it does not begin to detest the snake after thinking the matter over. It detests it *at first sight,* and devours it.

When I saw the Hindus and the Moslems, I understood at once what a strong temptation it was to the Moslems to give the Hindus a good licking, and the pleasure the Hindus took, on the sly, pitching a dead dog into Moslem mosques.

Now for those who have not seen or have not felt this, various explanations, coming from far back, may be found.

The Arabs, Mohammed's people, have set their mark on the people who have adopted Mohammedanism: Turks, Afghans, Persians, Hindus converted by force, Ethiopians, Moors, Malays, etc.

With the Arab, all is anger. His creed is full of threats: *'There is no other God than God.'* His creed is a retort, almost an oath—he scolds. He gives no quarter.

His greeting: May salvation be to whomsoever follows the *true* religion. (The true religion! To others no greeting.)

An Arab garden is a lesson in austerity, cold and rigorous.

The desert is the Arab's nature and all other nature is dirty, anti-noble and disturbs his mind. No painting, no flowers. 'All that is weakness.'

Uncompromising. In the old mosque at Delhi two brass idols were to be seen attached to the stones which formed the floor, in order that they be trodden under foot *ipso facto* by every one of the faithful who entered.

In the North, a few Hindu orphans embrace Christianity. The Moslem himself is unconvertible. The God of the Moslems is the most absolute. The other gods crumble away before him. And you humble yourself in the dust before this God. You throw yourself down, forehead to the ground. You get up again, and then throw yourself down, forehead to the ground, and so on.

The Arab tongue is a suction and expulsion pump; it contains ululating *h*'s which could only have been invented out of petulance and the desire to rout the enemy and one's own temptations.

His writing is an arrow. All alphabets are composed of a letter occupying a space either with crossed strokes (Chinese)

31

or with enveloping strokes (Hebrew, Sanscrit, Mexican, etc.).
Now, Arab writing is a single flight, a line made of lines. In
the ornamental writing, it goes all in arrows, very straight,
from time to time crossed and slashed by an accent. This
writing, which is really short-hand, is four times more rapid
than Latin writing (the Turks, who have just changed their
alphabet, have found this out to their cost).

The vowels do not count, only the consonants; the vowels
are the fruits and joys of evil. You do not note them, you slur
over them and they are pronounced almost like a muted *e,* a
letter of ashes, retained because there was no way of erasing it.

Thus the consonants do all the work. The consonants—
nothing can be said against them; they are privation.

The Arab is noble, neat, ill-tempered.

The Arab allegory is pruned down, there is nothing left
of it but a kind of terseness, the right word, a tense situation.
. . . Brief sentences, a brief sparkle.

The allegory is hurried.

The interior of a mosque is empty, it is a colored prison.

The Arab is courageous and chivalrous.

In every one of his virtues he is the opposite of the Hindus.
One has only to count them over.

★

Though not half as inoffensive as the Armenians and the
Jews, the Hindus, on the whole, are a prey. Alexander the
Great, the Greek kings, the Huns, the Mongols, the English,
the entire world has beaten them; it is eight centuries since
they lost their independence.

Even today, one Gurkha (a descendant of the Mongols

living in northeast Bengali) can master ten Bengalis and make a hundred of them tremble.

The explanation of all this is not so simple, yet one feels it distinctly.

The reason for it is, first, the spirit of natural defeatedness that is deep-seated in every Hindu. As soon as a royal elephant turns on its heels, the whole army goes to pieces.

Of course, you can never count on an elephant. A firecracker puts him to flight. He is calm. But he is not cool at all. At bottom, he is excitable. When things are not going well he gets panicky, and then it takes at least a building to hold him down. Even when he is simply rutting he loses his head. Everybody get out of the way! There's going to be trouble. Mr. Elephant wants to make love.

Besides, like all weak people, he is vindictive. Better say nothing about the look in his eyes. Any man who is fond of animals is disappointed in his expression.

Imagine an army of five thousand elephants, of as many and more chariots, of six hundred thousand men (that is the kind of armies Alexander had to contend with, as had quantities of conquerors), and you will understand what a bazaar this must have been.

How the Hindus enjoy this abundance (the more the merrier: like the gods of the gopurams), but a little army of ten thousand infantry scatters them into flight.

In addition to that, the Hindus, in the old days, used *shantras,* or magic formulae.

The value of magic is not to be denied, nevertheless the results are unsatisfactory. The psychic preparation is slow. A man kills more quickly by a stroke of the sword than by magic. His sword he can use at a moment's notice; he is not obliged to arm himself and to sharpen the edge every time he kills an enemy. Any imbecile who comes along can use a sword, and it is easier to assemble twenty thousand imbeciles than twenty good sages.

★

The Hindu adores everything. This is not his only sentiment.

He establishes communication, affectionate, fraternal, submissive or tender, with all creatures and transfigures them.

When the Bengali marries, it is not enough for him to put a string with a little gold jewel around the neck of her who will be his wife, which is the sign of married women, and a symbol of marriage. No, he *places this little jewel* on a coconut in a vase filled with rice, and he *offers to it a sacrifice of incense,* then he begs those present to be so kind as to bless this jewel. Next, the wedded couple together touch the salt, the rice, the daily food.

Once a year the plowman assembles his plow, his rakes, his hoe, and he bows down to these humble companions of labor, reveres them and begs them to kindly continue giving their assistance.

One day at least the plow is the master and the laborer is the servant. The plow receives the homage with its habitual immobility, and in this manner each worker assembles his tools and humbles himself before them.

The Hindu has been very careful not to establish relationships on an equal footing between himself and others. If he sees a superior, he bows and with his forehead touches the foot of the other.

His wife *adores* him. She does not eat in his company. But he, on the other hand, venerates his child; they have not that male and female look that one sees in the best society in Europe and which is the horror of today. He calls his son *papa*. Sometimes, even—delicious submission—he calls him *mama*.

The Hindu prays to everything. He who does not practice prayer lacks something (to pray is even more necessary than to love).

★

The Hindu excels in giving a special value to things and to actions. He enjoys making vows.

At Chandernagor I saw a young man and a girl, married twelve years ago to a day, who had made a vow of chastity for a period of twelve years. A conscience director, seated on the ground between the couple, seated likewise on the ground, made a little speech. . . .

I stole a look at the bride, I looked at the bridegroom.

Never, never had I really seen in India a young woman of perfect beauty. They run fast along the road to old age, and somehow, in spite of their modesty, they have an air of defeat, or, well, I do not know what. But with this one, there was an extraordinarily joyful sense of initiation. Something exquisite, very pure, neither thin nor ascetic, that filled her, that she retained, yet it flowed through her. And he had a rare beauty, and rarer still with a Bengali, he was affectionate, modest and reserved. Both in fine health, her age perhaps twenty-four years, his twenty-five years. I shall always see them. Their reserve that was so touching. Think of it, twelve years together, so young, so 'attractive,' and loving each other; here was joy unheard-of, quite Hindu, that I would have liked so much to have known.

★

Who has not read those novels in which, on account of a word omitted, of eyes that did not look up at a certain moment, two hearts that loved each other are separated for years? The young woman wanted to say 'yes,' she wanted to smile. . . . One does not know why she was disturbed, and now it will take three hundred pages to straighten out the affair. When it was so simple in the beginning, so simple. . . .

The Bengali takes it as a matter of course. Rather than interfere too soon, he prefers to accumulate disappointments. When they are love-smitten (in a Bengali film), the director has the greatest difficulty in putting it across. They do not look back, nor smile, nor make the slightest sign, nor do they blink their eyelids; they only move a little more slowly than usual and they go away. So when it means finding the beloved apparition again, obviously he has his troubles. They do not inquire. No, they prefer to ruminate. It is plenitude, the rest doesn't matter; they will lose the desire for food and drink, but they will do nothing. A word would suffice to prevent a lot of misunderstandings. No, they will not say it. They even choose misfortune, so attractive to them is a situation *involving density*. They like to feel it is the great act of fate rather than their small personal act. They breathe seven times before speaking. Immediacy they do not want. When you have a certain distance between you and the act, between you and your gestures, unhesitating though you may be in character, you will never get there 'in time.'

They are incapable of making a precise sign to signify 'yes.' They do not nod the head. They give a kind of swing of the head, starting from below, describing a part of a circumference from the left downward, then upward to the right. A gesture that seems to say: 'Ah! eh! after all, taking everything into account, if it can't be avoided, for want of a better solution, well, then.' Ask them if they will accept a *lakh* of rupees, or if they are truly Brahmin. You will not get a decided 'yes.' It will always be a long *yes,* undulating, yet dreamy, a swan's neck 'yes,' barely rid of the negative.

At Chandernagor, I took a wicked pleasure, when my cook brought me a meal, in looking severely at the dishes; he would then begin to prowl, ill at ease, in a perfectly useless manner, scattering or assembling the dishes, pushing them aside, drawing them one or two inches closer to each other. Ah! it was a sight, and when I had almost finished eating, I would stop with the same look; he would then begin again to try to find out what was wrong, doing nothing efficacious whatsoever, altering the position of the saltcellar vis-à-vis the oil cruet, and the dessert spoon vis-à-vis the plate, or gently rubbing a bit of the tablecloth, then another bit of it. This would go on for twenty minutes, I swear. And one could see that he was weighed down with embarrassment. However, he would never have said: 'Well, what is it? Is there anything lacking?' No. Interference like that would soon take all the weight of reality from life.

Why does this remind me of the game of flying kites? The Bengalis, who do not play, play at flying kites, even men of twenty-five. You should see them, these grave grown-ups, on the roofs of their houses playing out the string, gazing into the sky at their far-off kites. They amuse themselves by breaking off the string of their neighbors' kites, thus carrying on, at a hundred meters in the air, combats which are hardly perceptible to the one who is responsible for them, and are decided by the wind and fate, without disturbing his lazy meditations.

★

Those who would like to get hold of a good bone on which there is still plenty of meat must reflect upon the attitude of *non-violence.*

Gandhi (who in this respect so closely resembles Lao-Tzu) has just demonstrated that this attitude is always new. It is also one of the most ancient.

First the founder of Jaïnism (one of the most important religions of India), who forbade any meals after sunset for fear that an insect might fall into the food and, unperceived in the dark, be swallowed by mistake and thus come to die.

Then Buddha, the man *par excellence* of non-violence.

A tigress is hungry, he gives himself to her to eat.

(Always that touch of sentimental foolishness, accentuated in the carvings, where the famished tigers may be seen following the tigress and watching Buddha while they calmly await their beefsteak.)

And where in the world will one find a king like *Asoka,* so grieved over a little war he had made that during his whole life he performed acts of contrition and did penance for it?

All their institutions bear the mark of this acceptance.

Hindu religion includes monotheism, polytheism, pantheism, animism and devil worship. He who can do so adores only Brahma, but if he is unable to manage with that, he has Kali and Vishnu as well; and if that doesn't do, too bad, but there are plenty more of them. And he has put *everything* into religion.

Nothing is to be found outside of it. The priest is a pimp and his temple is full of women; union with them washes away all sin. The *Kamasutra* is not a book to be read *sub rosa.* I myself saw in Orissa and Kornarak on the façade of temples a half dozen love postures of which I had had a very hazy notion up till then. These statues are placed in evidence right on the exterior; the child who does not understand has only to ask the meaning, but it is usually obvious.

All actions are sacred. One thinks of them without being detached from the All.

The sexual act, even these very European words themselves, are already sins, infection, beastliness, human mechanism.

The Hindu is never apart from his sexual organ;* it is one of the centers upon which he bases his equilibrium. The same with the abdomen, the same with the forehead. He prays seated, his thighs open, on the ground, in a low equilibrium close to the lower center.

In France you tell dirty jokes and you laugh at them. Here you tell them, you absorb them without laughing. You follow them dreamily, you seek the game of organs.

In the Hindu songs, or dramas translated into French, there are always passages put in Latin, on account of their . . . immodesty.

In one of the best plays of Kalidasa (or is it in the *Malati Madhava* of Bhavabhuti?), after several passages that are so irresistible in their appeal to sentiment that one cannot help weeping, the young maiden involved in the affair is asked by her lady companion: 'Dost thou feel in thy vagina the moisture that precedes love?' Now really, that is the way one would speak of a mare in heat. Nevertheless, the young girl replies without astonishment, after the pretty fashion of young girls: 'Ah! Hush, how canst thou read thus in my heart?'

* *Sperm puts the Hindu in a state of mystic jubilation. He sees his goddesses covered with it. (See Atharva Veda, Book VIII, hymn IX.)*

39

Whereupon the European feels himself getting quite red in the face. For he is repressed. He lacks total equilibrium.

In the Hindu's love, there is something settled, perpetual, *constant,* not spasmodic. All Europeans have been disappointed in their intercourse with Hindu women.

★

'To arrange the world of creatures and of things, and of feelings, without breakage.'

Monotheism is violence. Even the Hindu who believes in one God recognizes several of them; he would not want to cramp anything at all: 'Come to me,' he meditates with open knees.

The Christian God—you have to bore your way through to him. The Hindu gods are everywhere. The Hindu does not kill, he wishes to live in peace with everyone (today ninety-five per cent of the Hindus do not eat meat).

Even the saint, he who has renounced, does not begin by doing violence to himself. Here is his life-table. Four successive states.

Brachmarya—Adolescence and its virtues of chastity and of obedience.

Grihasta—Marriage—life in common. Social life.

Vanaprastha—Progressive detachment.

Sanynasa—Life of renunciation.

One sees how carefully nature is handled.

The obstacles to holiness are in fact: (1) ignorance, (2) sexual curiosity as opposed to natural love for the woman and for the family with its natural responsibilities, (3) curiosity concerning the world.

Their gods behave like heroes or like men. They have not

done violence to themselves. They are men with magic powers. But they have no moral elevation. They are not known for their abstemiousness; only the saints of the highest order are like that, and in fact, the gods are overthrown by them.

Siva was making love to his wife when two gods, Vishnu and Brahma, I believe, entered. Does he stop? No, indeed, he goes right on. He had been drinking a little. Vishnu and Brahma went out. Siva recovers his self-possession and asks what has happened. He is told. He then says these profoundly human words (I quote from memory) concerning his 'nature' as one used to say: 'And yet, this also is my true self.' And continuing: 'He who will adore it, it is myself he will adore.'

And today India is full of *lingams*. There are hundreds of millions of them, and not only in the temples. If you see more-or-less polished stones set up under a tree, that is a *lingam*. They are worn as a necklace in a small silver case.

At first even the institution of caste may well have been a formula that permitted everyone to live without denying himself anything, and sharing, as it were, in divinity—the result, in fact, of being in the service and under the orders of the Brahmins.

As for the 'outcasts,' and for the great shame that caste has become today, it would be well to remember, concerning them, that good Samaritans are very rare in India, more so than elsewhere, and that the Hindu adores keeping someone under his heel.

The Hindu has always had a desire to merge all the gods, all the religions. He succeeds in doing so in Southern India and Ceylon.

But when it comes to the Moslems this is not so easy. The Moslem says: 'There is no other God than God and Mohammed is his prophet.' That settles it.

41

And then there are the Christians. But the Christians are active white men, conquerors and missionary-born, delighted with the words: 'Go and evangelize the earth.' It is they who endeavor to convert the Hindus. Notwithstanding, the latter are still seeking a universal, all-embracing religion.

Vivekananda is willing to go so far in psychic science as to seek the ecstatic union by means of the Moslem, Christian, Buddhist, etc., technique. 'And he succeeds in doing so.'

★

A man traveling for the first time in India, with not much time to spare, should be very careful not to spend it on the railway.

Twelve thousand kilometers are not unusual—nor are they obligatory.

He will regret that the intellectuals from whom he might get some excellent information live in the cities, he will regret it, but he will not linger there. And in the villages he will pray and meditate.

He will limit himself in the use of lamplight. Preferably he will use the dark as much as possible.

And above all he will get it into his head, once and for all, that he is an alcoholic, and if he takes no alcohol, that he is an alcoholic without being aware of it, and that his sort is a thousand times more difficult to treat.

He need seek no further—meat is the alcohol.

If the stares of the natives annoy him, he will not lose his temper, he will not say: 'Those mules' eyes make me furious,' he will know that their eyes annoy him because they have in them an element that may be elevated or not elevated, but which he *does not grasp*.

42

He will get it carefully into his head that meat is an evil, an evil determined to come out into the open. It comes out in gestures, wickedness, work. And cursed be these three!

He will be wary of the egg, which is not so inoffensive itself, with its own form of aggression ready to be launched.

He will learn how to sit down in a way denoting acquiescence, not criticism and an air of always being on the defensive.

He will fast, remembering the words of Mohammed that fasting is the gate of religion, and he will live by his lungs, the organs of complete acceptance—(what you do not eat, you must breathe).

He will absorb the air, the pure air, the air that escapes, the expansive air, the air without a face, the unlimited air, the air that belongs to no one, the virgin air, the intimate air that nourishes without interfering with the senses.

To inhale it is nothing, expelling it is all, into the centers, the lotuses, the centers of the abdomen, the proud centers, the frontal center of white light, and into the thoughts, into the friendship of all the thoughts and into the beyond of thought.

★

The Ganges appears in the morning mist. Come, what are you waiting for? Adore it! You must do so, isn't it obvious?

How can you stand there upright and stupid like a man with no God, or like a man who has but one, who clings to him all his life, who can neither adore the sun nor anything else? The sun mounts on the horizon. It rises and stands straight up before you. How is it possible not to adore it? Why always do violence to yourself?

Come into the water and baptize yourself, baptize yourself morning and evening and undo the cloak of stains.

Ah! Ganges, great being, who bathes us and blesses us.

Ganges, I do not describe thee, I do not draw thee, I bow down to thee, and I humble myself under thy waves.

Fortify in me renunciation and silence. Permit me to pray to thee.

In India, if you do not pray, your journey is in vain. It is time thrown away.

The decency and modesty of the Bengali women and young girls, which is often so irritating to Europeans, is nevertheless admirable and restful. Covering a part of their faces with a veil as soon as they catch sight of a foreigner, and above all, immediately leaving the middle of the pavement and walking on the extreme edge of it—compared to them, European women seem w . . . . s. I who had found the English woman reserved. In comparison to the Hindu woman, woe is me, shame on them, with their breasts visible, their legs almost bare, with nothing to protect them, they might even be touched by a passing dog.

And they look at you, mind you. They do not look down. They do not hide their faces. They look at you. And then their breasts are in evidence, ready for who knows what attack.

I was present when a factory (a jute factory) was letting out workmen and women. The latter hardly spoke, they were distant, and very proper with the *sari* wrapped around them. What deportment!*

Each one in herself. A Hindu crowd is always amazing. Each one for him- or herself. As in Benares, in the Ganges, each for himself and looking after his own salvation.

---

* *And yet, as soon as they become workers, their reputation is gone. Deservedly, so one hears.*

To the Hindu, religion matters and so does caste—the rest is mere detail. He bears clearly and distinctly on his forehead, in big horizontal strokes of cow dung, the signs of his cult.

To the Hindu, regulations and the artificial are what count.

One must say, with wants as meager as his have always been, this orientation seemed inevitable. When the European reaches the point of satiation, he rests, but the Hindu has no wants. It is all the same to him if he takes one meal or three; one day he eats at noon, the next day at seven o'clock; he sleeps when he happens to be sleepy and wherever he happens to be at the time, on a blanket laid on the ground.

Nothing in the way of poverty and distress can astonish him.

One should see the hotels they have there. Diogenes thought himself so clever because he lived in a tub.

All right! But he never dreamed of letting it to a family, or to some travelers from Smyrna, or of sharing it with friends.

Well! in a Hindu hotel you are given a room with exactly enough space for a pair of slippers. If a dog were put in there it would suffocate. But the Hindu does not suffocate. He manages with whatever volume of air he is given.

Comfort upsets him. It is inimical to him. If the people who conquered him had not been such a reserved people as the English, the Hindu would have made them ashamed of their comfort.

Nothing in the way of suffering either will astonish the Hindu.

Now a poor blind man in Europe arouses 'noticeable'

compassion. In India, if he thinks he can count on his blindness to move people, just let him try. No, if, in addition to his blindness, his knees have been crushed, an arm cut off, or at least a hand, and let this be as bloody as possible, and then a leg missing and his nose eaten away, even that goes without attracting attention. A suggestion of St. Vitus dance in what is left, and now, perhaps, there may be some use in showing himself. It will be admitted that his situation is not all that could be desired, and that a little penny might give him pleasure. But one cannot be sure. These sights are so ordinary, so numerous. Their emaciation is sometimes such that one wonders whether it be that of a man or of a skeleton.

There is a beggar with no hands and paralyzed legs who goes in the morning from one end of the Chowringhee (the grand boulevard of Calcutta) to the other, pulling himself along on his knees with a sack tied by a rope to his loins dragging two yards behind him. You might think he made 'big money.' I had the low curiosity to follow him for half an hour. His winnings, in all were two 'coppers' (there are four coppers in an anna and sixteen annas in a rupee of seven francs). Some of them totter scarcely a yard in a morning, falling down and getting up again. In the same city live the rajahs, the richest people in the world with the American millionaires. No, no, each one his destiny. One adjusts oneself to it. When an egoist becomes a bigot, he becomes a hundred times more egotistical.*

I was ushered one day into the office of a Hindu lawyer in Calcutta.

* According to the Hindu doctrine it is useless to render material aid to someone, while spiritual aid must really be rendered, and even so it is very difficult. Dhan Gopal Mukerji defines a hospital thus: a solid house of disappointment where men delay the evolution of their soul by doing good.

46

I have no particular statement to make regarding him. He is an eminent man and well known in the law courts.

I would like, however, to touch on the subject of his files. On some shelves bundles of dirty linen were to be seen. These were not bundles of dirty linen, but files, squeezed into old hand towels, from the holes of which protruded, here, the signature of the clerks, there, words of minor importance. Some of the papers were slipping out and waved gently in the draught.

Needless to say that, from the judicial point of view, I shall be most careful not to open my mouth.

As to the other points of view, I will confine myself, for the present, to some reservations.

I was able to see other houses that did not belong to lawyers. If only they had been empty! But this ugliness, this rococo!

For a marriage, they spend up to fifty thousand rupees (half a million francs). And it is hideous.

In India one can get used to eating nothing but rice, to not smoking any more, nor drinking alcohol nor wine, to eating very little.

But to be surrounded by ugliness—one can go no further in austerity. It is very harsh.

Why so much ugliness?

Here is a people three thousand years old, and the rich man still has the tastes of the parvenu.

★

A Western philosopher who was passing this way felt overwhelmed by a feeling of pantheism, due, he thought, to the heat and to the neighboring jungle, and so was enlightened as to the profound causes of Hindu religions and philosophies. It was inevitable, one could not be anything but a pantheist in this climate.

If that writer happened to go to the banks of the Maranon (Upper Amazon) and of the Napo, where it is very hot also, and where there is a real jungle, he will, no doubt, be surprised to find Indians who are light-hearted, lively, cool, precise, and not at all given to pantheism.

Besides, India is not such a hot country that you are obliged to eat under a shower bath there. There are four rather cold months. In winter, when you perform your ablutions in the Upper Ganges, you shiver. In Delhi everyone coughs. The head of Dupleix College in Chandernagor wears an overcoat.

As for the jungle, it is a luxury that the Hindus who are fathers of large families can no longer afford. They have reduced it to a bare minimum. They have put rice fields in its place.

The trees that one sees in the north are rare, isolated, tall, with immense and beautiful foliage in the shape of a parasol. They give the country a look of great peace and majesty.

It seems more likely to have been the famines (if the rains are late in the summer, famine is sure to come), the innumerable diseases and the snakes, rather than the severe heat, that have had an effect on the Hindu, not exactly making a pantheist of him, but making an impression on him such as the sailor might have at sea, and giving him a kind of defeatism.

Yet certain tribes, most of them much older than the Hindu, real natives such as the Santals, have none of the Hindu characteristics. Nature has influenced them in a quite different way.

Moreover, it is not the jungle that makes the tiger, but the tiger who chooses to go into the jungle. It also lives in the mountains, in the coldest weather.

All peoples seem to choose a certain type of country to settle in, though they may prosper in several.

The Portuguese in the plains (Portugal, Brazil), the Spanish on high plateaus (Mexico, Peru, Ecuador, Chile, Venezuela, etc.). The Arab is more like himself in the desert (Arabia, Egypt, etc.). It so happens that the cactus (on the plateaus and pampas of South America) is the tightest, the most unapproachable plant, just like the Indian of the same countries.

Most of the trees in Italy are taller than those in France. As soon as one reaches Turin the difference is striking. The leaves of the chestnut trees are heavier in Brussels, lighter in Paris—and as a rule, all the vegetation in the Paris region and Brussels shows a slight tendency of the same kind. Does that simply imply that the Belgian prefers to see good stout chestnut leaves to more delicate ones? and that he chose to live in Belgium for that reason?

Does it mean that it is the sight of the heavier vegetation that has rendered his mind . . . a little less nimble and a little more fleshy?

Does it follow that drinking the water from the same soil as the plants, surrounded by the same humidity, the same wind, the same tone, and in short, eating qualities of the products of the same soil, he has grown somewhat like them also?

No, one cannot say this, it is much more complicated.

★

India sings, do not forget that, India sings. Everywhere, from Ceylon to the Himalayas, they sing. Something intense and constant accompanies them, a song that does not 'detach' them.

Can one be entirely unhappy when one sings? No, there is a cold despair that does not exist here. A despair without hope of issue, and with nothing to look forward to, that is to be found nowhere but among ourselves, and of which the hero of Knut Hamsun's *Hunger* would be a typical example.

The Asiatic is a born student. Bengal is swarming with students, with matriculated students. The Chinese knows nothing but *examinations*. Examinations make the mandarin of every class.

The Asiatic knows how to accept, to be receptive, to be a disciple. I was present in Santiniketan at a lecture on a Vedic text. Good, but nothing exceptional. The students were there, ready to accept everything. If I had been the lecturer, I would rather have liked to insult them.

In their literature, in the dramatic works of Bhavabhuti, Sri Harsha, Kalidasa, in the *Tantchatantra* and in many of the Chinese works there are three lines of quotation to ten of the author.

It is a question of showing what a good pupil one is.

If someone in Bengal meets you, knowing you are a writer: 'So you have done the Humanities. What degree have you got?' He asks you that at once. Naturally you must say 'Doctor' and if you are a pork-butcher, say doctor of pork-butchery. They asked me besides: 'Who is your master?' When I replied: 'Well, nobody; why?' they did not believe me. They imagined it was some kind of trickery on my part.

★

What I can never get used to is seeing them grovel in

front of me. No, I am not a *rajah,* nor a *nabob* nor a *zemindar,* nor a great nor a small lord, I am like everybody else, you hear me. May I not be reborn a groveling Hindu! Be simple, I pray you, there is nothing extraordinary about me, neither you nor I; it is no use throwing yourself on the ground. No, I do not need any servants. (A 'cook' all the same succeeded in getting himself hired. What style! He might have been serving a king.)

Servants have always been terribly painful for me. When I see one I am overwhelmed with despair. It seems to me that I am the servant—the more he humbles himself, the more I am humbled. In fact, everyone has noticed that people who have a houseful of servants, whether they be dukes or maharajahs, end by resembling servants. They never have the look of free men.

Ah! They can be proud, the Brahmins, of their fine work. During three thousand years, they have succeeded in degrading two hundred fifty million men.

This result, unique in the world's history, is enough, it seems to me, to disgust one with the *Laws of Manu,* with their two weights and two measures, and with *Hindu religion,* double-faced, one for the initiated and the other for fools.

Humility is certainly a quality of the highest order; but not degradation. Not very long ago an Untouchable who was about to cross a road had to ring a bell and cry loudly: 'Beware, Brahmins anywhere about here, a wretched untouchable is going to pass. Beware of the outcast who is going to pass.' Then they stood back, or had him devoured by the dogs. This poor devil who could only despise himself, but who, though crushed by his situation, had still not reached the point where he was unable to find the 'real God.'

But so abject a situation *completely* soiled the Brahmin.

51

To bear such groveling on the part of a human being, to oblige him to do it, one must be very base oneself, firmly set in baseness and ignorance.

Now the situation is changing. Jealous as hunchbacks, but always as ignorant as carp, a hundred times less representative of the real India than simple weavers or members of middle or inferior castes, they are beginning to find that these are standing up to them. *Ranassanry naiker d'Erode,* founded at Madras, is the *self-respect association.* Suffice it to say, the Brahmins are not admitted to it.

In the Presidency of Madras they hardly dare to travel on the railway. As soon as they are seen arriving with their famous cord around their waists, they are questioned, their untold stupidity is put to the test. They are soon left 'à quia.'

Really, I shall be glad to see India again a few years from now. I shall meet some humble people there.

At a university where they were supposed to be very anxious that the West and the East be brought closer together, an eminent Hindu Sanscrit scholar was begged by one of the greatest connoisseurs of the music of Bengal, of the north of India and of Nepal, to translate for the European public the following words of a song: 'Does one cast pearls before swine?' The answer was as follows: 'It is thanks to this conception, Professor, that pearl experts, who keep pearls too long, turn into swine.'

It is thanks to this conception that they have maintained ignorance and misunderstanding of their own religion among two hundred fifty millions of their people.

He who after that speaks of the humanity of the Hindu speaks another language than mine.

★

Do not think, either, that the Hindu is crushed under the load of regulations, nor is his religion tyrannical *in that way* as it is so often said to be.

The Hindu is naturally delighted with regulations. Those of religion are insufficient, he only asks for more to follow.

Even in love, he is delighted to follow regulations (Kamasutra).

Even as a thief, he is delighted to follow regulations. In an old play (by Kalidasa, I believe) where the thief tries to enter a neighboring property, from which he is separated by a wall and a door, there he is, complacently going over the code of robbery, its different rules, stopping finally at rule number six, namely, 'rules to follow in the case of burglary added to housebreaking.'

A Hindu friend, if I rendered him a service, usually gave me next day by way of thanks a wretched bunch of flowers (in India they do not know how to arrange a bunch of flowers but they offer them all the time, to open the conversation) and a few rules, such as to raise the right foot in order to breathe to the right, never to urinate without breathing from the left nostril, to insert the little finger into the ear after sunset, etc.

I am so sorry that these rules are not worth the trouble of following. I would have very much liked to have been for once in good hands and under foreign and safe guidance.

In France, a poet who has become almost a national figure is often invited to speak on every subject. And upon my word, he accepts. He will speak about everything. Everything thinkable that can be extracted from a subject, in spite of his ignorance of it, he extracts. And it cannot be denied that he makes one think, though generally about something quite different.

The Greeks were the same (not only the Sophists).

But the Hindu is superior to them all. With him, emptiness does not exist. Ignorant of a subject as a stone, he will embellish it at once.

His natural history, which contains very few good observations, does not fail to enumerate eighteen ways of stealing, seventeen of falling down, eleven of getting up again, fourteen of running, and fifty-three of crawling.

Eighteen *verbal* manners of stealing naturally, without a sketch, without a detail, but eighteen and not nineteen. *Eighteen* and the question of stealing has been dealt with to one's entire satisfaction.

★

Adoration, like love, presents a fatal downward slope. He who lets himself go goes far. . . .

You adore? Well! Give us some proofs!

Here is where the sacrifice comes in, the 'palpable' part of adoration.

God listens absentmindedly to prayer. But let blood be spilled for him, and he draws near. He is obliged to come. One can catch him with a victim.

The Hindu is particularly attracted by sacrifice.

If he offers up a goat, it is because he is not allowed to offer up more.

There was once a caste that spread all over India, its one aim being to supply God with human sacrifices. They caught you on the road, carried you before an altar, and squeezed your neck. God, who apparently accepts everything, said nothing. And, content, they went off again to seek another man. Thus it was that several travelers stopped sending news of themselves to their families and relatives.

I wonder whether the following trait is connected with religion: the Hindu has a propensity to strip himself that is as natural to him as sitting down. Everyone, at certain decisive moments, is aroused to fight or conquer. The Hindu is aroused to drop everything. Before you can say 'Jack Robinson,' the king leaves his throne, the rich man strips off his clothes, abandons his palace, and accountant of the Chartered Bank of India his post. And not for anyone's benefit. (It is curious, I never find the Hindu kind; he is not occupied with others, but with his own salvation.) But it is as if his clothing or the display of his wealth chafed his skin, and the more naked and the more abandoned he is, wandering and with no one in the world, the better that will be.

Next come the austerities, and I am almost inclined to attribute his austerities to wickedness.

I will not mention fasting. He fasts as others would eat. If he succeeds in something, he fasts; if his calf is sick, he fasts; if his business is going badly, he·fasts.

★

In addition, you have their vows. God does not speak first. God lets you come and go. But you put a chain around your arm, and you throw him one end of it, then what can God do? That is the way one hopes to tie him up.

Nowhere have I seen people making vows as in India. If you see a Hindu not doing such-and-such-a-thing, don't worry: it is a vow; he has stopped smoking: a vow; he eats eggs, he stops eating eggs: a vow. Even the atheists still make them. To whom do they offer them? I suppose that the mere binding of oneself, of uniting oneself to the years, that extraordinary immediate and constant extension is an enjoyment for them.

The Hindu adores possessing self-control (that is to say, having himself well in hand), a word that he uses even more frequently than the word 'to adore,' and he smacks his lips over it.

★

If there is a creature that the Hindus hold sacred, it is their mother. Where is the ignoble individual who would dare to say a word about her?

I have a good mind to be that ignoble individual.

—That would be the last straw.

—Obviously.

But now, I am really sorry, for if there is a creature in India who works and is devoted, who knows from practice what it means to *live for others,* it is the mother.

No, decidedly I will say nothing against her.

I say only, something that is universal, that the women preserve the existing order, be it good or bad.

If it is bad, that is a pity.

And if it is good, that, probably, is a pity too.

In India, as elsewhere, the idea is growing more and more that it is the next generation that matters. In the old days one sacrificed oneself for the preceding generation, for the past; now it is for the future.

One of the most amazing sights I saw was the belly of my *yogi guru.*

He caught his breath in a manner that was high, slow, and as though drained. He drew it into himself through the chest, the belly, and piled it up almost between his legs. Several of his teachings I am only beginning now to understand—at the moment I was hypnotized by his belly, the belly suddenly appearing swollen as though harboring a head or a foetus and being slowly reduced.

In fact, the inhaling lasted fully eight minutes. He took great care not to injure himself, for the breath can give a dangerous wound like a knife.

This extraordinary man, whose superb chest swallowed up quarts of air, which he then distributed into his soul, who seemed rather young in spite of his eighty years, had nothing of the saint about him either. He was above human misery, inaccessible rather than indifferent, with a kindness that was almost invisible, and also perhaps a slightly pained look like those persons who are suffering from gigantism, or who possess more talent than personality.

★

The Hindu is often ugly, with an ugliness that is vicious and poor. The sparkle in his eye may be deceiving at first. But he is generally ugly. He does not photograph well, his plays, his films bring out, for those who have not observed him calmly enough (curious to say, he has an air about him that disguises everything) the ugliness of his features, his whole aspect with that vicious, rotten look on his face, so characteristic of him.

Certain old men are beautiful; indeed, their beauty is incomparable. In no other country does one see old men with majesty such as theirs. Rather like old musicians, old fauns, who know all about life but have not been deteriorated, nor even excessively affected by it. But they grow beautiful.

For the Hindu and the Bengali, between eight and sixty is the awkward age. He looks silly. Life is for him the awkward age—the head of Tagore at sixty is splendid, absolutely splendid. At twenty it is a head that is not alive enough, that has no impulse, and that is not yet sufficiently rested, not wise enough, so truly is wisdom the Hindu's destiny.

They were right to persuade the Hindus that they must attain wisdom, or holiness. From a study of their physiognomy alone, I would have given them the same advice. Be saints, be sages.

Those degraded, degenerate faces, that silly look, those low simpleton's foreheads—but I am not making it up. Open a magazine, *The Illustrated Weekly* or any other—that impertinence, the shamelessness (they absolve themselves of everything), the air of greed (when they *are* greedy) (no, trade does not suit them either!) (the Marouaris 'would sell their mothers' milk' to make money, says the proverb), a look of conceit, flashy, pretentious, egotistical, makes millions of faces ugly. The worldly and powerful in India seldom have beautiful faces. I only saw one, and it was absolutely dazzling. I suppose that it is because of this vigorous plenitude of beauty when it is to be found among them, and then it is really exceptional, that they have always been called good looking.

What spoils their faces more than anything is the pretentiousness. What spoils their apartments more than anything is pretentiousness (seven or eight chandeliers in a room otherwise empty and unattractive, no, really it is not pleasant) and it spoils ninety-nine per cent of their decorations and their epic poems as well.*

Well, if you haven't perceived how ignoble his face is (when he is not a saint or a sage), and if that has told you nothing, go and see a Hindu film (not Bengali), but do go, and see ten of them while you are about it, so as to make no mistake. Here, the still water begins to move, and you will see everything. Faces becoming bestial and angry—you will see how one flagellates, how another smacks and strikes as if it were of no importance, how one tears off an ear, catches hold of breasts, unconcernedly spits in a face. You will see how a 'nice' young man behaves in this way, quite unaffectedly, right before the young girl he loves. How a prince imprisoned under a divan can be crushed carelessly little by little; how an ill-tempered father throws his son on the ground, or has him shut up in prison; not to mention the carefully thought-out and executed martyrdoms, where cowardly creatures slobbering with sadism display that puffed-up, unspeakable ignominy, where even the honest(!) resort to duplicity.

Treachery, knavery, base actions, here you have their whole drama. Big, hydrocephalous heads, the enormous heads of *Mantek* eaters, of the mentally backward, with the small foreheads of habitual criminals. They show in Marseilles some 'special' films, naturally forbidden by the police in ordinary picture houses. But nowhere have I seen sadism as continual and as natural as in Hindu films, and I have seen a good fifty thousand meters of them. Their supple way of smashing a hand was so 'enjoyable' that I, who have long since stopped

* *The lowest theater with unspeakable 'sickeningly sweet' scenery has its two spotlights so that the false diamonds and the glass trimmings may have the proper glitter.*

Take away the fawning praises, the flattery in Hindu literature, and a third of it would disappear completely.

blushing, blushed and was ashamed. I was guilty, and I shared, yes, I too shared in the ignoble pleasure. ,

★

The Hindu does not kill the cow. No, evidently, but everywhere you will see cows eating old newspapers. Do you believe that the cow is naturally partial to old newspapers? This would be saying you don't know the cow. She likes green grass, which is good to crop, and, in a pinch, vegetables. Do you believe that the Hindu is ignorant in the matter of the cow's tastes? Come, come! After five thousand years of living together! Only he is as hard as leather, and that's that.

When he saw Europeans looking after animals he was amazed. When a dog goes into a kitchen, one must immediately throw out all the food, and wash the pots; the dog is impure.

But, pure or impure, he does not like animals. He is not fraternal.

One day, at a Bengali theater, I saw a famous social reformer impersonated—Ramanan or Kabir himself who, in some century or another, tried to do away with caste. Some individuals of different castes came to him. He blessed them all equally and prevented them from bowing down to him, then all the other characters raised both arms and sang of the equality and the fraternity of men.

This sounded false, false! Every five minutes they raised their arms to the sky. The audience was delighted. Yes, they raised their arms to the sky, but they did not stretch them out toward one another. Ah! no! nothing like that—lame, poor, blind, get along the best you can. How false it all sounded, and how it was applauded.

Everybody knows these poets who, year after year, pile up thousands of verses, with a tear in every one. All very fine, but try to borrow a penny from them, just to see. The 'poetic faculty' and the 'religious faculty' are more alike than one would think.

★

What a pity that instead of the lungs it is not the heart that can be exercised; you have it there in your breast for life, and good will doesn't change it much. It is the cause of good will and ill will. What enthusiasms we would have if we could manipulate it! Physically manipulate it!

Alas! The fact is that some objects will have to be found that are worth enthusiasm.

★

It is very difficult to judge an opera from the libretto and a song from the words. The words are only a support.

That is why Homer is difficult to judge. All the more so is the *Ramayana*.

When reading it, one thinks it boundless, every piece of it boundless, too huge, a great part of it no aid to the comprehension of it as a whole. But if you hear the same pieces sung, what was too long turns out to be precisely 'what matters,' now becomes a superhuman litany. And this, one perceives, is where demigods are an advantage. Achilles is but a man, Roland is but a man. But Arjuna is god and man. He intervenes for and against the gods and the sun is a mere soldier in the affair.

When the combat is not going as well as he would like,

61

the hero, having shot 'twenty thousand arrows in one morning,' retires under a tree to meditate, and beware! when he returns to the fray with his psychic power and his bow.

One day, in a little town, I went into the courtyard of a house, and saw six men naked to the loins, Sivaists, who were seated on the ground, around books written in Hindu, with the expressions of bulldogs tearing a piece of meat apart, holding little cymbals in their hands, and madly singing, in rapid, diabolic rhythm, a damnable song of sorcery that took hold of you irresistibly, that trumpeted, was ecstatic, overpowering—yes, the song of the superman.

On account of songs such as this, one throws oneself under the wheels of the chariot of the gods at the October festival. I myself would likewise throw myself under the wheels for such a song. Song of the psychic affirmation, of the irresistible triumph of the superman.

Now that song was the same *Ramayana* I had found so unnecessarily long and boastful.

*

In this courtyard there was a very old man; he bowed to me, but I perceived the bow too late. The music was resumed and I said to myself: 'If he would only look at me again!' He was a pilgrim, not from this region. It seemed to me that he felt friendly toward me. The music ended. I was transported. He turned in my direction, looked intently at me and went away. In his look there was something for me, particularly. What it said to me I am still seeking. Something important, essential. He looked at me, me and my destiny, with a sort of acquiescence and rejoicing, but through it ran a thread of compassion and almost of pity, and I wonder what that means.

I have here in Puri province of Orissa somewhat the same impression that I had in Darjeeling; an immense relief, as soon as I meet other men than Bengalis. But it is in Bengal that I preferred to stay and I was always convinced that when I returned to France I would miss them a great deal, and already in this place I miss them. I left Bengal two days ago and regret it. Here there are charming people who smile at you . . . well? But there, one went about in the 'dark.'

★

The God of the Hebrews was far away. He revealed Himself on Mount Sinaï, from afar, in lightning and thunder, to one man alone, and all this in order to give him ten commandments graven on stone.

One day His son was incarnated. From that moment a new era opens in the world. Nothing is as it used to be. A sort of enthusiasm and security invades the world.

But for the Hindu, in whose country one does not have to wait twenty years for a god to be incarnated, Vishnu alone having been incarnated twelve times, this is nothing. He feels extraordinarily at home with his gods, hoping to have them for sons, and the young girls for husbands. Also the *shaktas* (prayers) resemble, in their familiarity, the worst prose, and even invective has a prominent place in them.

★

When you ask a southern Hindu the names of the gods who figure on the *gopurams,* there are sure to be some among them whom he does not recognize. 'There are so many of them,' he says, and then one sees on his face that particular smile of the sated rich man, who does not have to deny himself anything, and you wonder whether feeling thus is not a necessity to the Hindu.

In the south, particularly, when you see the hundreds of gods with ominous faces in the temples, the separation between the religious conception of the West and that of the Hindu seems an abyss.

It is a religion of demons, you say to yourself, that is obvious.

Now when you read the *Ramayana,* you see that three quarters of the book are composed of villainy and of the supernatural powers of villains, demons, hermits and inferior gods, all busy most of the time doing evil, or at war, controlled with difficulty and inefficiency by the big gods, who are plainly improvident and irresponsible. But then, what is the difference between gods and men?

It boils down to this: *They possess magic power.* As they are bad, there is probably exactly the same proportion of badness as in the Hindus; they use their magic power to do evil, for their cupidity, for their concupiscence, and that with vile cunning.

Now, any other people would be revolted. Not the Hindu. *Psychic power* is all that counts. The ideal, even up to a few years ago, was to acquire a mastery over psychic forces. A man who can destroy a palace by magic, a man who can weave a spell, has always been considered by them the *ne plus ultra.*

Even one of the greatest saints, and one of the most moving in the world, Milarepa, began with black magic; at eleven years of age, in a spirit of revenge, he destroyed crops by making hailstones fall on them, and threw toads and monstrous beasts around, destroying a house and those who lived in it.

He began that way; that is the rule. Then he expiated himself, and the tale of his expiation is beautiful indeed. The Hindu has psychic power and he makes use of it. But kindness with him is rarer than elsewhere. To do harm by psychic means is his first temptation. To do good is an exception.

★

An aquarium is usually composed in Europe of a very large quantity of receptacles, of pools and of glass cages where you find what you have seen everywhere and even on your plate. In fact, they are labeled 'trout,' 'perch,' 'pike,' 'plaice,' 'carp' three months old, carp one year old, carp two years old, etc., sometimes a catfish and when they want to make a splurge, a king-crab, an octopus and two or three sea-horses.

Now the aquarium of Madras is *quite small*. It has only twenty-five compartments. But perhaps two of them, at most, are insignificant. And nearly all of it is stupendous.

What fish can compete in strangeness with the *Autennarius hipsidus?* A big good-natured head, a gigantic philosopher's head, but where as much learning can be seen in its chin as in its forehead, an enormous wooden shoe of a chin, not very prominent but very long. Two fins, just like forepaws, on which it squats, and plays the toad or the wild boar. If it moves them from right to left or against the glass, its paws become real hands with forearms, weary hands, that can do no more.

It has a comb on its nose, it is the size of a frog, yellow like a flannel vest and of the same texture, with even little stitches to be seen; one wonders how it happens that this plucked chicken is not eaten up immediately by its neighbors.

It remains squatting for hours without moving; it has a stunned look that betrays it.

For if a prey does not pass in front of its mouth, it will not bestir itself. But if it passes just in front, then, yes, the jaws open, snap up, close again and go 'clack.'

When the female lays eggs, four meters of gelatin and of eggs come out of her body.

Most of the *Tetrodon* species have difficulty getting people to believe at first sight that they are not artificial and entirely made up of either morocco, or of pajama material, or, the finest ones, of tiger-cat's fur or of a cheetah's skin. They have such a stuffed, swollen, shapeless look, like goatskins. But these goatskins are dreadful (*Tetrodon oblongus,* Karam pilachai); as soon as one among them shows signs of either slight fatigue or illness, they surround it, catch hold of it, some by the tail, others by the front fins, hold it firmly while the rest tear pieces of flesh from its belly as hard as they can. It is their great sport.

You will never see one among them with a whole tail. There is always some famished sadist waiting to take a bite out of it before the other can turn around.

The *Mindakankakasi* has an oblong spot in its eye.

First it has a very beautiful black pupil, then on top of that a spot, a very large stripe of dark blue, a somber canal that goes all the way to the top of the head.

And when it is sick, it cannot keep itself in a horizontal position. It advances head downward, the tail just touching the water.

66

The scorpion-fish is a fish as far as ten little parasols joined to a little body can make a fish; also it is infinitely more cumbersome than any Chinese fish.

Then there were two extraordinary fishes whose names I could never discover. One with eye-sockets that are developed like Neanderthal Man's, another slightly less, with an extraordinarily human look, of the Caucasian type (the fish, on account of the absence of eye-sockets, are usually more similar to the Mongolian races). And a well-cut mouth, fine and almost spiritual, and it shows its teeth, or rather a horny little tonguelet that gives it a kind of pout. The fin along its back, when at rest, is folded four or five times. And there are twenty others that seem quite new and to have sprung from the unknown.

★

Certain people are surprised that, having lived in a European country more than thirty years, I never happened to speak of it. I arrive in India, I open my eyes, and I write a book.

Those who are surprised surprise me.

How could one not write about a country that has met you with an abundance of new things and in the joy of living afresh?

And how could one write about a country where one has lived, bound down by boredom, by contradiction, by petty cares, by defeats, by the daily humdrum, and about which one has ceased to know anything.

But have I been accurate in my descriptions?

Let me suggest a comparison.

When a horse sees a monkey for the first time, it observes it. It sees that the monkey tears flowers off bushes, tears them deliberately (not abruptly); it sees this. Also that it often shows its teeth to its companions, that it snatches their bananas, though possessing as good ones itself, and lets them fall, and it sees that the monkey bites the weaker ones. It sees it caper and play. So the horse forms an idea of the monkey. It forms a circumstantial idea of it and sees that itself, the horse, is quite another creature.

The monkey still more quickly notices all the characteristics of the horse, which not only make it incapable of hanging from the branches of trees, of holding a banana in its paws, in short, of accomplishing a single one of the acts that the monkeys consider so attractive and in which they excel.

This is the first stage in knowledge.

But in time they begin to rather enjoy meeting each other.

In India, in the stables, there is almost always a monkey. It renders no service, apparently, to the horse, nor the horse to the monkey. Nevertheless, the horses who have a companion of this kind work harder, are more willing than the others. Presumably, with its grimaces, its capers, its different rhythm, the monkey is restful for the horse. As for the monkey, it would be glad to spend a quiet night. (A monkey who sleeps among its own kind is always on the *qui vive*.)

Thus, one monkey is more enlivening for the horse than ten or so horses.

If one only knew what the horse thinks of the monkey at this moment, quite probably it would say: 'Ah . . . dear me, I'm not so sure.'

Knowledge does not progress with time. Differences are overlooked. You compromise. You come to an understanding. And you cease to come to conclusions. This fatal law acts in such a way that the permanent residents of Asia and the persons who are most thrown together with the Asiatics are not at the exact point where a focused vision can be retained, whereas a passerby, with his innocent eye, is able sometimes to lay his finger on the center.

★

If you read *Hind Swaraj,* by Gandhi, and after that any political writing by any other man in the world, you will find a fundamental difference between them. In *Hind Swaraj* there is holiness, there are undeniable traces of it there. Gandhi when young was fussy and argumentative and vindictive and carnal, more concerned with what was upright than in being really upright. He has grown better. He has truly searched for God. He has his day of silence in the week, of silence and meditation. It is for this day of silence that so many Hindus love him, and for that I also love him.

Certain people maintain that he is naive when he declares: 'If some English citizens afterwards want to remain in India, let them keep their religion, let them live in peace, but *let them no longer kill oxen.*' I was extremely touched by this. To believe that some Englishmen could deny themselves beef for the sake of a foreigner, you must really be a man who believes in the spirit of conciliation. You could never meditate enough upon this spirit.

Alas, Gandhi for the Hindus is only a stage.

As a matter of fact, they do not want him any more. The people want him. But the intellectuals are far beyond. They have tasted of the European fruit.

European civilization is a religion. No one can resist it.

The most popular thing in Benares is the cinema. And what films!

In twenty years little will they care for the Ganges.

The white peoples' civilization never tempted any other people in the old days. Almost all people do without comfort. But who can do without amusements? The cinema, the phonograph, and the train are the real missionaries from the West.

The Jesuit Fathers in Calcutta make no converts. Among their advanced students not eight per cent are Christians. But all are converted to Europeanization, to civilization, and they turn into communists.

The young people do not bother with anything but America and Russia. Other countries are for pleasure trips, countries without a creed.

They say that all European science originated with them (algebra, etc.), and when they put their minds to it they will make ten times more inventions than we do.

One must not judge a schoolboy too hastily as long as he is in 'harness.' He is not his real self. Now the Hindu has been under foreign domination for eight centuries.

I am convinced that once the Hindus are in power, in ten years the institution of caste will disappear. It has lasted three thousand years. It will be swept away. But it is a job that must be done at home, and that a foreigner cannot do.

★

In India there is undeniably a color prejudice. The Hindus cannot stand the Whites. As soon as they see us, their faces change. In the old days, probably it was the opposite.

In America, there are some twenty races; in spite of that,

the American exists, and more distinctly than many a race that is pure.

Even the Parisian exists.

With all the more reason, the Hindu. Gandhi is perfectly right to maintain that India is one, and that it is the White people who see a thousand Indias.

If they see a thousand Indias, that is because they have not found the center of the Hindu personality.

Nor perhaps have I found it, but I feel sure that it exists.

HIMALAYAN RAILWAY

When you arrive at Siliguri, you see, on a couple of very narrow-gauge rails, a tiny, tiny locomotive, what I might call a pony-locomotive, which appears to be harnessed to a little train.

Now you are puzzled. What! would it dare to undertake, does it really promise itself to undertake to climb the Himalayas?

And besides, it is divided in two; one half holds a little coal, and it is the other half that must do all the work.

There are some very small cars there, too, of a size to match.

Lastly, you may be able to see the steps (so-called). A weasel, at a pinch, might use them.

A hatrack was not omitted. You can, to be sure, deposit a box of lozenges on it, or some packets of ten cigarettes.

Even the lighting has not been forgotten. But the bulb is missing. So small it was, judging by the socket, it would not, all the same, have given any light. So it was better to do away with it. Far better.

A cattle car, very suitably, is hitched to the train, and certainly there might be room in it for a basket of poultry and a quarter of a dozen lambs.

There, the locomotive is off, and its tactics at once become visible.

In the first place, nowhere is there any sign of a tunnel. For such a small locomotive, it would have been ridiculous to dig tunnels and to spend money, so they simply made a path, a well-trodden path, a little apron of mountain earth, and then on you go. Thus the travelers get all the view they could desire.

It takes curves the way one would take them cycling; it is never at a loss. It goes forward, goes backward, describes circumferences and little roundabouts, and retraces its steps.

If you get off at a stopping place, two small Nepali women, smiling, a gold coin in the nose, and so charming you would give them your soul, offer to carry your luggage, and under your enormous valise they keep on smiling.

Everywhere smiles, little, precise, aerial, the first smile of the yellow race that I have seen, the most beautiful in the world.

And one wanders about among prayers on slips of paper attached to the trees.

The Himalayas with their snowy peaks appear.

All the same, the famous Thomas Cook and his accomplice the American Express should not try to make us believe, as they insist on doing, that it is the most grandiose railway in the world.

One moment, Thomas—now that you are making comparisons—just go on an excursion to the Cordilleras of the Andes, and cross the Guayaquil to Quito. When you have seen the jaws of the *Chimborazo* and of all those monsters, the

Cotopaxi, the *Tungurawa,* always ready to bury you in their lava for a hundred square miles, inhabitants included, then you can talk. For about twenty hours you go along on the black earth, the hard lava, in amongst the assembled volcanos.

And the condors are quite as good as kites, I think.

But I do not wish to find any fault with *Kinchinjunga* and its group. Enormous, one must admit.

★

All over the world one can make oneself understood by gestures. But in India, impossible.

You make a sign that you are in a hurry, that one must be quick, you wave an arm in a manner that the whole world understands, the whole world, but not the Hindu.

He does not take it in. He is not even sure it is a gesture.

How oppressive, too, is their mere presence!

What a relief to find oneself with the Nepalis, when one sees a smile, the natural smile that comes to you, that awaits its happy return from you, and begs you to disimpregnate yourself, to leave off, in charity, your meditation.

That smile of the Nepali, the most exquisite one I know, exquisite, not excessive, not disturbing, but delighted, undissembling, pure.

The tropics are full-blooded.

The mountains are pure spirit. Hands have ceased to serve as an intermediary. Play of hands, play of villains.

The eye alone sees it. The mountain is freed from dirt, from the senses, from the slime of vegetation, from odors.

The Hindu, in fact, is aware of it. And whoever desires holiness 'finishes up' in the Himalayas.

The Nepalis have chosen to live in the highest country in

the world. Among them, the few visible Hindus, even the mendicant friars, the Gurus, the saints, appear as rubble.

★

The Nepalis are the opposite of the Hindus.

The Gurkhas, stocky, tough Mongols despising the Hindus and waiting for the first chance to pitch into them.

The Tibetans, like the Nepalis, are the opposite of the Hindus in quite different ways.

The Hindu is handsome and feminine. The Hindu woman's inferiority is, in the first place, amazing. One might imagine oneself in an insect world: she is a head shorter than he.

And the Hindu shuts her up in the house. One does not see her. He is everything. She is nothing. I managed to see some Tibetans who were not the ordinary type of Tibetan, the latter being of a much more delicate build, and they were quite remarkable. Thus:

The Tibetan, male, was heavy, big, tall and not handsome, but rough.

The Tibetan, female, was heavy, tall, not beautiful, almost always strong and tough.

Some of these Tibetan women of the old type married as many as five men (at a time, naturally), and I have an idea she made them toe the line. If anyone had to be shut up, it is more likely to have been the men.

I saw one of these women who held the purse-strings and, with great assurance, ordered her meek, strapping, six-foot males about.

★

When something goes wrong with a Hindu, even if he is rich, married and the father of ten children, he says, 'All right, if that's the way it is, I am going to beg.' He entrusts his fortune to his nephew and goes off to beg.

This is an accepted custom. Arriving at certain crossroads in life, he has but one thing left to do: begging, or rather, to live by begging.

The Hindu begs coolly, with conviction, with cheek, considering this employment to be his destiny. The Hindus (the Hindu is neither kind nor charitable) go their way and leave him, for it is his destiny.

The Brahmin who begs comes in without saying anything. If one gives him no matter how little he says nothing, but if you show the slightest impatience he will curse you unto the fifteenth generation. Then a whole flock of goats would not suffice to remove the curse.

Too late, the gods, who were waiting, immediately set to work speeding catastrophes on their way to the curse.

In Ceylon, a young man on a bicycle passed me at full speed. But a minute later he was beside me, holding his bicycle by one hand. He held out the other, 'poor boy, no money.'* He had a marvelous brand-new bicycle with a gear box. He seemed to be in good health, young, and enthusiastic, I was very glad to be able to assist him.

Oh! that I might one day beg in a car, and meet a compassionate soul!

The Nepali begs with his smile. He looks so happy over your meeting. It is a very personal pleasure—it is really *you*

* *(In English.)*

79

whom he is delighted to find. So how can one refuse him?

(I am speaking of the children. The Nepali is not given to begging more than other people.)

Small coins are rare in India. When you see them, a kind of mild convulsion of the heart seizes you.

The impression of having a beggar in front of you is always painful. A pool of injustice that you cannot define.

With the Nepalis, begging is done so simply and fraternally. He begs from you today. Tomorrow it will be your turn; between us we can always manage.

The Tibetan priest begs with delicacy. He goes to the market, stands in front of the vendors, a tiny drum in his hand, as tiny as a mango, to which are affixed two little red strings holding a light ball of red thread. He shakes the drum from right to left, the little balls strike the drum; at the same time he shakes a tiny bell. He then accompanies this so very abridged orchestra by a song, weak and secret, indistinct, breathed rather than sung, a sort of plaint in sleep; this lasts a minute.

His begging bowl catches a few vegetables and a handful of rice which he places in his sack, then he passes on to the next vendor, thus making the rounds of the market.

Simple, discreet, inaudible save to the one concerned, I shall always hear that distressed sigh, restrained, delicate as though coming from a sick person who, with his lungs gone, wants to sing a last time.

A voice that might be passing gently through the bleeding bronchial tubes, or again, as if one had taught a dog to sing, who would learn and repeat his melody without too rashly forsaking his habitual sighs, those disturbing sighs that they give when they are asleep, caused by cares that seem familiar to us.

Voices like their eyes . . . pleated. Like the formulae in the prayer mills, another form of discretion.

But if you go into a monastery of lamas, or into a temple, where they spend the whole day, one sleeping and eating, while it is the other's turn; and if you hear them singing prayers, mumblingly, bent over enormous loose-leaved books as large as valises, you would cease to recognize them. Deep voices with notes lower than those of the famous Russian basses; a kind of belching and obscene singing, that makes one turn back to see if it is not gross mockery and grotesque imitation. No, indeed, it is their grumbling everyday voice.

They have also an instrument, a sort of trumpet four and a half meters long, which they turn on the countryside to call people to prayers. A noise as from an enormous hippopotamus-like glottis comes from it, and this sound, excessively loud anywhere else, weak and obscure here in the Himalaya mountains, passes over the hamlets like a sigh.

SOUTHERN INDIA

The Southern Hindu, belonging to the Dravidian race, small, lively, quick-tempered, no longer corresponds in any way to the European conception of the Hindu.

As soon as you reach the South, the skin gets darker, and you are dealing with almost black people. Dressed accordingly: pink and red disappear, and dark green and violet take their place.

The big â, ô, and ê of the Northern languages disappear; everything moistens into consonants in Malayan, or is buttressed by double consonants, in Tamil (Tamil is a more ancient language than Sanscrit, and has nothing in common with the latter). The people here are no longer 'important.' They look at you with an expression that is of no consequence. No hypnotism at all. They are not ruminants. If they have two minutes to kill, they do not squat down. You see some of them standing up or even walking, fast.

In the temples, the gods form a façade, their *gopurams* are bazaars for gods, demons and giants.

All the gods are a bit devilish. You throw yourself at full length on the ground for them, and rather quickly (quite unceremoniously). In front of Ganescha, you give yourself two small blows with the fist near the ear. They have a preference for the gods of lesser divinity, for example, the goddess of smallpox. Religion loses its beauty, its peace. It has ceased to have a fine sound. They are multi-theists.

Often, at the same time, they are converted to the Catholic faith (the only part of India where converts are numerous).

The English look on them as children.

These are the natives of India, the real ones. They occupied the whole of India in the past. They were colonized by the Northern Hindus.

It is hard to say what they might have been without the influence of the conquerors and of their religion, in which they are completely wrapped up as they would have been wrapped up in any other religion.

They were people who particularly liked the magic* of words.

At one period alone (that of Sangham) they mention 192 poets of merit: fifty-seven farmers, thirty-six women, twenty-nine Brahmins, seventeen mountaineers, thirteen foresters, seven merchants, thirteen Pandyas kings, etc., a potter and a fisherman.

*Magic in the full sense of the word; the reading of the RAMAYANA TULSI DAS absolves from all sin.

This Tulsi Das, who had written the RAMAYANA and the adventures of HANUMAN and of the army of monkeys, though indeeed a poet, was put in prison by a king.

He meditated in his prison, from his meditation came Hanuman and an army of monkeys who sacked the palace and the city and set him free.

And now let us have a contest: Where is the European poet who could do as much? Who is there that can bring forth as much as a mouse for his defense?

★

It is impossible to think of India without being a Communist. The social question is perhaps only of secondary importance. But the degradation, the lack of human dignity which results from a society with two different standards is such that the whole man is corrupted by it in all that he is, says and does, and he who is honored (the Brahmins and the rajahs, and perhaps all of us) even more than he who is held in contempt.

★

However, there is not another country in the world where, to 'get into conversation' with you—in a train, no matter where—the native speaks to you . . . about Jesus Christ.

The Hindu is quite unable to imagine that a man could be indifferent to religion.

Most of them sincerely love Jesus Christ, regret that he was not incarnated among them, regret that he was not incarnated a second and a third time, would like to have news of him.

Nevertheless, even a European atheist is often hurt by the familiarity with which they converse about Jesus Christ.

★

My Bengali companion said pleasantly of the women in the South: 'A thousand coming, not one pretty.' He should have said: Ten thousand coming, not one pretty. (Finally, I saw one.)

As for the men, stubborn heretic faces, some with profiles

and eyes like lizards (particularly when ill, they resemble lizards). Nose, eyes, mouth bunched together as if the result of a curse or of a cataclysm. Low foreheads (a frontal ribbon, one might say), and the skull with its bushy hair (but he is shaved to the top of his head) make his resemblance to a monkey more striking.

A lot of Bourbon heads too, but reduced, feverish, the power lost, and the hair worn in a bun.

Their curiosity is greater than that of the Northern Hindus, which is already so great. If one of them gets hold of the slightest bit of information about you, that you are thirty-two years old, for example, he immediately informs the entire neighborhood, all the travelers at the station, all passers-by in the city. Not only that, but from a distance he is questioned. And he replies triumphantly: 'He is thirty-two years old. He has come to visit India.' And the amazing news spreads like wildfire.

They look at you as one looks at a new arrival at the zoo, a bison, an ostrich, or a snake. India is a zoological garden where the natives get a chance to see, from time to time, specimens from elsewhere.

If a European is questioned on his return from India, he does not hesitate; he replies: 'I have seen Madras, I have seen this, I have seen that.' But this is not so; he has been seen, much more seen than he has seen.

★

When the Hindu talks to you, it is nose to nose. He takes the breath from your mouth. He can never get near enough. His big Jupiter-like head and his disinterested eyes are wedged between the horizon and yourself.

So, holding you down, he unrolls his phrases, he declaims. All this in order to say perfectly insignificant things. But he is driven by a strange force to make a speech, preach a sermon, and a piece of information at once takes on the importance of a matter of universal interest.

The Southern Hindus, in the villages, when you stand still a moment, surround you ten deep, enveloping you with their eyes, so close that if you cough you injure two or three of them.

If you speak, they somehow manage to get closer. The Northern Hindu declaims, the Southern Hindu roars.

Not only is his singing (that of the Dravidian populations in the South) high-pitched, but also his speech. With regard to French, if he speaks it, he has the firm-set notion that it is a language of the head, and only by extreme force and in the throes of anguish can you hope to extract more or less of it from up in the top of your skull. You always feel like saying to him: 'Calm yourself, calm yourself, really it will come out!' But, helpless with rage, he is carried irresistibly on.

★

The Tamil language is composed of words having, on an average, six syllables. Several have fourteen. When there are less than four syllables it is not a word any more, but a detritus. The English language seems to them a ruin. What are all those senseless little bubbles called the preposition, the article, etc.?

Tamil is an agglutinating language. You solder everything you can together. One word is made out of three.

In this way, though it is slightly more complicated, no doubt, the ten or fourteen syllables are formed.

These words are borne away at top speed. You touch the first syllable and you go galloping off. When you get to the end, you can take a rest. That is where little gaps in the conversation occur. However, some go at such headlong speed (most of them) that they do not stop. So you listen to this marvelous mechanism which, at a superhuman pace, accomplishes its natural purpose, without faltering.

They pronounce the words as though they were having a fit.

An unhappy childish haste, which is to be found again in the fixed expression of their eyes, fixed, yet at the same time making haste, making haste to see, making haste to see what? And doomed, obviously, to failure, though you do not know why.

When they sing, their song is like a hanging. They sing only to hang themselves, and high. They make straight for the most inaccessible notes, without a springboard, hang on in despair, and wavering between two or three higher notes, remain there crying, suffering, objects of pity, ready to let themselves be cut in pieces; but why? Then, all of a sudden, they stop short, and leave the mortal terror of the air above, then there are two minutes of silence, and up they climb again, or to be more exact, there they are again suddenly, more immensely unhappy than ever. And their tortures go on like that sometimes for over an hour.

They also adore a sort of oscillating between low and middle notes. They introduce an unbelievable number of words into an already rapid cadence, forming a recitation multiplied by four, the best thing that was done in the way of motion before the locomotive. And all this is not in the least disagreeable, ending in a little point that is rather mediocre, sourish, unsoaring, and quite like an operetta.

★

When it comes to speed, they have nothing to learn from anyone. Into their drama, which is more varied than anything of the kind in Europe, they introduce everything—the nine ingredients, comedy, morality, poetry, action, etc. The play goes on without interruption for seven hours, through from two to two hundred and fifty scenes, and heaven knows how many changes of scenery. All this with a style and with gestures that are merely suggested, and at once forgotten. The whole thing is diverting, full of life.

The cinema taught them nothing. They were already much faster. The gags are followed by bursts of laughter in the house, loud, but immediately after gobbled up, swallowed, vanished. Discharges.

There is a power in all this that says: 'Come on, don't dawdle, cut it short!' Someone sings, the same song is taken up at once in another key. Then suddenly the melody is broken off altogether, and then the key is changed again. The actors go out, leaving no atmosphere behind them. The scenes pass rapidly by in the natural chronological order, following each other very closely, and a donkey could understand it. As there is no atmosphere, interruptions are of no consequence. On the stage, a man reduced to extreme poverty begs for charity. A fellow, in jest (they all have a sense of the comic; many of the scenes are extraordinarily droll), a fellow in the orchestra seats throws him an *anna* (a sou), and immediately the whole house amuses itself throwing *annas*. This lasted, I am sure, from eight to ten minutes, then began all over again.

Another time I was present at the last performance of a theatrical troupe. They were giving a drama with a tendency to moralize, and its subject was poignant.

91

Well, right in the middle of the dialogue, the audience got up on the stage (generally children, and several of them at a time) to present flowers and garlands which the actor at once put around his neck, and oranges which he stuffed in his pockets, or as far as possible kept in his hands, and the performance went on.

Extremely embarrassing custom to the European—the feminine roles are played by men dressed as women, a kind of abortion, most of them, with at times a beautiful contralto voice in falsetto.

'These roles,' as someone in the audience explained to me, 'could not be played by women. They are too difficult(!). The young men that you will see have practiced from their earliest years to learn how to be effeminate. And a man who practices goes much farther than a woman.'

Here, indeed, I said to myself, are arguments. But when I saw the actors, I was not too disappointed. They had in fact many feminine reflexes, every instant, even when standing apart, of which a woman is neglectful, if I may say so.

But make-believe cannot have the value of the natural.

I saw afterwards, in Madras, Sundarambal, the great Tamil actress, a marvelous singer, the only beautiful Dravidian woman I ever saw, and one most truly talented. She seemed to have oil as well as blood in her body, and petroleum. When she appeared, she crushed the other women (who were men) even before she had made a gesture (she made few), before she had begun to sing. She possessed a wholesome femininity, that of a woman made of glands and soul. The others were coquettes, for the man cannot be a natural woman. They were trying to be *women*. She was trying to be a human *being*. She succeeded, without doubt. But existing in her was that essential, peculiar something, all the more exciting in that she paid no attention to it—femininity.

★

His rhythm alone would make the Southern Hindu more akin to the European than the Bengali.

The modern Tamil novels are like European novels—plenty of action.

The people of the South are not unlike the Italians (there are, in fact, a good many of them in Madras) and the Spanish.

They have a nice sense of the comic, and no European could ever ridicule caste institutions and their 'sacred customs' as do the Tamils today, and with matchless comedy.

And besides, they enjoy (contrary to the people of the North) seeing European films.

It is obvious that they do not want to set up *their* truth against that of European civilization.

(The same thing with the Negroes of Africa, and the same thing where their rhythm is concerned, and the ease with which they are Europeanized.)

While for the Bengali, unadulterated European culture will never be his culture. He will make something quite different out of it, and certainly quite remarkable.

★

I wonder whether the Hindu race, without its gift for the psychic, would have gone in so much for the occult.

Though many Hindus who have a European education have lost their metaphysical gifts, others, particularly among underlings, having not done much studying, and thus been less exposed to mental distortion, have retained them.

There was an employee of the South India Railway who, they assured me, cured snake bites.

As soon as someone was bitten, a relative ran to the station: 'Where is so-and-so?'

'Oh, he is on the train, on the . . . line.'

They telegraphed to him: 'So and So. Snake. Bitten.' The telegram flew from station to station in search of the train and the man.

They waited anxiously for the reply. At last it came: *'He will be all right.'** And everyone went away rejoicing. And the poison was no longer effective.

What did the employee do? Well, he communed with himself for an instant in a compartment. 'In the name of . . . (one or another of the saints) may the poison not rise.' Then he went on punching tickets.

Hundreds of telegrams were exchanged thus, and quantities of venom turned to water.

Psychic gifts of a similar kind are to be found among all castes, the noblest as well as the most despised, even among barbers and cobblers.

You can understand how, in such a country, the distinctions between imbeciles and non-imbeciles are so unsatisfactory.

The employee mentioned was perhaps mentally an 'imbecile,' or even amoral, as often happens with them, but, nevertheless, making more complete use of the resources of the total *being* than his superiors.

In India, the critical mind is not what counts.

* *(In English.)*

But is the critical mind anything to gape at?

Pilate had a critical mind, a distinguished mind. Even with Christ, he succeeded, after a fashion, in appearing to be the cleverer of the two. 'What is truth?' said he. And then exited. He was, in fact, referring to a mental truth. In this domain, one could not give him what does not exist.

★

The less approachable someone is, the more he has an inner life.

Such is the Englishman, and such the Bengali.

One cannot too strongly urge translators with the 'gift of tongues' to set to work on Bengali.

There is no literature so amazing and often so beautiful as Bengali literature. Tagore is not a lost islet. There is a quantity of writers, there are hundreds of works of the nineteenth and twentieth centuries to translate, for which I would exchange half of Europe's literary production.

The poems, the novels, the prayers are easily translatable and have an irresistible appeal.

Each time I read a Bengali writing, after ten lines I am caught.

There is in Bengali literature something true, entirely true, and it is neither the holiness nor the truth, but the inner life.

When you read a Bengali, you cannot help loving him.

He moves, he is important. You are not obliged to stoop. You do not perceive, in reading him, that slow rhythm that is so annoying in his films. I, for one, do not mind. But the most indulgent Europeans have never been able to sit through

an entire performance. Yet, if interest in knowing came before the pleasure of seeing the beautiful, one would have a
cinema in Paris where Bengali films were shown. Those who
want to think would find something there.

A BARBARIAN
IN CEYLON

The best-known son of the kingdom of England, Thomas Cook, starts out on the principle that, if you travel, it is in order to see great monuments, very old and well catalogued, and to stay quite near by in a great palace, very modern, provided with an excellent restaurant where you have a large number of dishes copiously served.

For he considers that no one would set out on a journey if he did not have a big appetite.

It is this same engineer-psychologist who declares with regard to Ceylon (a property that he has been managing for forty years, to everyone's satisfaction. Even the prisoners there have the eyes of gazelles, and the woodcutters the arms of a young girl. He calls the tigers by their names):

'On a surface of 25,331 thousand meters, it would be hard to find assembled a larger number of natural, archeological and picturesque marvels, etc.'

Now then, Thomas, no doubt, but make a final effort, please squeeze in a bit more.

★

The Cingalese walks reverently. He is reverent. One day, by mistake, I went into a corridor that led to a *very large hall*. Religious sentiment reigned here. At one end of the hall there was a crowd, motionless, contemplative. I went forward. They were watching a game of billiards.

One day I was passing in a *rickshaw* through a street in the native quarter. A clamor stopped me. I got down. The noise came from a Catholic church, with all its doors open. I went in. They were reciting litanies, with such faith, with such feeling, that it was extraordinary. From time to time one of them would go up and massage one of the glass cases enclosing a small statue of a saint. He would magnetize it (all the little statues were shut up in glass houses, otherwise by the end of a few days nothing would be left of them), so he would massage it, then pass on to the next, and then another of those present would get up and ingratiate himself in the same manner.

They were visibly at home. Several were wandering among the altars in the side aisles, with palpable adoration. They were fingering the altar-cloths, the flowers, the chandeliers, with devotion resembling addiction. To tell the truth, this religion seemed to suit them. In the temples of the Buddha, they have nothing to do.

A Cingalese, one Sunday, came to harass me on my bench. He wanted to explain to me the merits of Christianity. I replied with those of Buddhism. But he would not listen. *The hope,* said he, *paradise with God immediately after death.*

★

It need not be supposed that all the Cingalese are slow.

Some advance in regular, almost rapid strides.

If, however, they give an amazing impression of inertia, it is owing to their lack of gestures. They talk to you without using their arms. Their arms, well, they are reserved.

The trunk immovable, undisplaced.

Tall, slender, delicate, serious, a kind of human stilts, nothing aggressive in their gaze, which one encounters like a far-off horizon, absolutely restful.

Feminine and like women who are afraid of disturbing their beauty.

Not liking to displace their center, nor to have emotion.

At a popular picture house, I saw an old Western film. Well, not for an instant did I get the impression of movement, of emotion, nor even an American impression.

This, for an astonishingly simple reason, merely that the film was accompanied by a constant pulse of formidable beats of a tom-tom, bang, bang, bang, bang, through which the religious sounds of a harmonium tried to pierce.

No other film gave me that impression of eternity, of endless rhythm, of perpetual motion.

They rushed stupidly about in this film. Nevertheless, the film was motionless. It was carried away by an immensity greater than itself, like a cage of fighting cocks in an express train.

★

Another thing regarding the speed of the Cingalese. You have probably seen, at least in atlases, those superb names, long, marvelous serpents with drumlike vowels: *Anuradhapura, Polgahawela, Paravanalankulam, Kahatagasdigilva, Am-*

balantola. Well, they say them so fast and so sweetly (they erase, rub out English, in the same way) that Anuradhapura makes something hardly more important than 'amena.' Excepting, however, the children.

Listen to them singing and reciting in school; here is the magnificent unfolding of the contemplative words, something that is well disposed, and well understood inwardly, as when the Russian recites his admirable polysyllabic words (but there it is the consonants that come out) and as the Greeks do also (the same love of redundancy, for the lengthening and the triumphant mastication of words).

NATURAL HISTORY

The bat is not a bird, if you like. But it can give all of them points in flying. You would think a pigeon was paddling, that it was beating the water, it makes so much noise with its wings. The bat no one hears. One would think it was taking to the air like a sheet with hands.

With its long beak and its torpedo-boat head, the crow is a black poltroon. In India, a quarter of an hour before sunset, it becomes voracious and, risking everything, hurls itself upon a piece of bread given by a timid little girl. This temerity is brief, and soon it flies away swiftly toward its nest, a hard nest and made without taste. There are tens and tens of millions of crows in India.

Ten minutes later comes the bat, here, there, where? silent, bewildered, with wings that weigh nothing and do not even make a sigh in the air. You hear a humming bird; but a bat, no. And it never crosses a space in a straight line. It follows ceilings, corridors, walls, it coasts. Then it is on a branch and in a twinkling is hanging from it by its claws, as if to sleep. And the silent moon shines on it.

★

It often amuses one to look at birds. They go away, come back, circle about: tricksters.

That is not the parakeet's idea of flying. Flying is the passage from one point to another in a straight line. Parakeets are always in a hurry, the rudder very straight (they have very long and strong tails), they go away without turning their heads, almost always two of them, neither wind nor shadows make them swerve from their course, and they chatter all the while.

★

The pigeon is sexually obsessed. As soon as it has swallowed a mouthful and has regained a little strength, there it is, back in the clutches of its demon. Its throat rattles (who ever called that cooing?), a thick rattle that would fluster a hermit, and at once the female responds, she always responds, even if she does not wish to be approached immediately—a rattle that overwhelms her, that is much bigger than she, and heavy, obese.

And they fly off, noisier than the sound of boots.

INDIA

Kites are big good-for-nothings. As long as they can make use of the winds, and lounge around, they are quite happy.

Even the crows, who are afraid of everything, attack the kites. I saw a couple of them who really did not know where

106

to go next. In the trees, the small birds attacked them. Crows chased them off a rooftop.

★

A mouse that is stalked by a cat can still escape. With a mongoose on its tracks, it can still keep a spark of hope.

But if a crow, perched on a branch, has noticed it, all is up. Diving almost on the perpendicular, or if the branches do not lend themselves to this, slipping down on a slant or even horizontally, it arrives, it is there, it carries it off. Fast though the mouse may run, it is like a man who is running swiftly, and is pursued by a plane. He is lost. He is irrevocably lost.

MALAYA

The red-beaked white-stoppers are lighter and better shaped than the sparrow, with feathers so close together no wind can lift them.

The red-beaked white-stoppers have a specialty. As soon as there are two of them installed on a branch (and when there is one, an instant later there are two of them) one retreats (oh, a very little retreat) sideways along the bough and without turning its head.

The other at once moves along (oh, a very little move) the same distance—an eighth of an inch.

They spend hours in this way. For a tree has more than one branch. As soon as a branch has exhausted its possibilities of fun, on to the next.

And no ugly chirping like sparrows; no, sometimes, rarely, a little 'tac . . .' to show that it is not an empty thing.

107

And though small, it has none of that epileptic headshaking that makes the sparrows so silly and so foreign to us.

ZOO IN SAIGON

The Jabiru does not eat a fish that is alive. He swallows it dead. He seizes it therefore, and clinches his beak on it, on the head, on the body, tosses it, catches it again, and again tosses it and recaptures it till it is dead.

There is the prudent Jabiru, and the imprudent Jabiru.

The imprudent Jabiru, that is to say, who is satisfied with a semblance of death (and beware of the bones of a fish that is alive and struggling in the stomach) is the one who carries it onto the pebbles where he gives it many a blow with his beak till it lies still. Then he eats it. But any experienced Jabiru knows that a fish that has stopped moving on the pebbles may not be dead, and may still be dangerous. That is why the prudent Jabiru dips it in the water, to test it, and in fact very often the fish is alive, and at once, though very slowly, hopelessly, seeks to abandon the scene and death. It happens also that a Jabiru is unable to get his fish out of the water, though he has given it many blows, but each time it falls back. Then all of a sudden, impatiently, he waves immense and noisy wings over the pond and he wonders, and you wonder, and all the other birds wonder what is going to happen.

A BARBARIAN
IN CHINA

The Chinese people are born craftsmen.

Everything that can be discovered by tinkering the Chinaman has found.

The wheelbarrow, the printing press, engraving, gunpowder, the rocket, the kite, the taximeter, the water mill, anthropometry, acupuncture, the circulation of the blood, perhaps the compass and a quantity of other things.

Chinese handwriting seems like the language of contractors, a group of workshop signs.

The Chinaman is a craftsman and a clever craftsman. He has a piano player's fingers.

Unless you are clever you cannot be Chinese; it is impossible.

Even to eat the way he does, with two little sticks, requires a certain cleverness. And this cleverness he has sought. The Chinaman could have invented the fork, which a hundred races have discovered, and used it. But this instrument, which requires no skill to manipulate, is distasteful to him.

111

In China the 'unskilled workman' does not exist.

What is simpler than to sell newspapers?

A European newsboy is a shouting, romantic fellow, who tears about, screaming at the top of his voice: 'Times. Herald-Tribune,' and gets under your feet.

A Chinese newsboy is an expert. He examines the streets where he is going on his rounds, observes where the people are to be found and, using his hand as a megaphone, lets out his voice, now toward a window, now toward a group there on the left, wherever it is necessary, calmly.

What is the use of letting your voice run away with you, tossing it where there is no one to catch it?

In China, you have nothing that is not clever.

Politeness here is not a simple refinement, left more or less to the judgment and good taste of each one.

The chronometer is not a simple refinement more or less left to the judgment of each one. It is a work that required years of application.

Even the Chinese bandit is a qualified bandit, he has a technique. He is not a bandit on account of a sense of social outrage. He never kills uselessly. He does not seek the death of people, but the ransom. He refrains from doing them the slightest bit more damage than is necessary—cutting off finger by finger and sending them to the family with demands for money and dark threats.

On the other hand, cunning in China is not associated with evil more than with anything else.

Virtue is the thing that is the most 'cleverly contrived.'

Take, for example, a corporation often looked down on: that of the porters.

Porters, the world over, usually pile up on their heads and on their backs or their shoulders everything they can.

They are not conspicuous for their intelligence. No, indeed.

Now the Chinaman has succeeded in making his job a work of precision. What the Chinaman likes more than anything is equilibrium. In a wardrobe, one drawer that balances with three, or two, or with seven. The Chinaman who has a piece of furniture to carry divides it in such a manner that the part of it hanging behind him balances with the part of it hanging in front of him. Even a piece of meat he carries dangling from a string. These things are slung from a big bamboo stem carried over his shoulder. Often you can see, at one end, an enormous saucepan, or a smoking kettle, and at the other boxes, plates, drawers. One can easily see what skill this requires. And the procession goes on throughout the Far East.

CHINESE TYPES

Modest and rather retiring, choked, one might say, phlegmy, the eyes of a detective, and on his feet felt slippers, and wearing them out at the toe, as is only natural; the hands in the sleeves, jesuitical—artlessness that is perfectly transparent, but would stop at nothing.

Face of gelatine, and suddenly the gelatine melts and out of it comes a ratlike darting glance.

With something drunken and soft about it; a sort of rind between the world and himself, and he detests water (excellent for the personality, in fact, is dirt).

Not yellow, the Chinaman, but chlorotic, pale, lunar.

In the theater, the men sing like castrati, accompanied by a violin that quite resembles them.

No enthusiasm; a language made up of monosyllables, the shortest possible, and even so there is too much of it.

Moderate, gently sad when in their cups, restful and smiling.

Even though the eyes and nose and ears and hands of a Chinaman are so tiny, they are not filled by his being. He leans far backward. Not at all by concentration. No, the Chinaman's soul is concave.

Rapid little gestures, but not hard, not even precise. No emphasis, nothing showy. Mad about firecrackers, he shoots them off on every occasion, and their brief sound, sharp without consequence and without resonance, pleases him (like the noise of the clogs that the women have on their feet).

He likes very much, too, the abrupt croaking of the frog.

The moon pleases him, the Chinese woman resembles it amazingly. That discreet clarity, that precise contour, appeals to him like a brother. In fact, many of them are under the auspices of the moon. They do not care in the least for the sun, that big bumptious fellow; they are very fond of artificial light, the oil lamps which, like the moon, throw a good light on them alone, and cast no brutal rays.

Faces astonishingly impregnated with wisdom, beside which the Europeans look exaggerated in every respect, veritable wild-boar snouts.

No debased types, nor mentally backward; even the beggars, though these are indeed rare, appear to be quite lively and good company and intellectual—many of them like 'fins Parisiens,' with an impression of frail correctness such as is to be found at times among the offspring of old aristocratic families weakened by intermarriage.

The Chinese woman's body is admirable, standing straight as a plant, never that bitch look European women are so apt to have, the old as well as the young with such agreeable faces, not extenuated, but alert and wide-awake, a body that always does its work; and their tenderness to each other and with their children is charming.

★

The Chinese has not exactly, as it is understood elsewhere, a religious mind. He is too modest for that.

'*To seek the principles of things that are hidden from human intelligence, to perform extraordinary acts that appear foreign to man's nature, these are things that I would not like to do.*' (Extract from a Chinese philosopher, quoted by Confucius with a satisfaction easily imaginable.)

Oh, no, he would be ashamed. He would not want to exaggerate. Imagine it! And then he is practical. If he bothers about anyone, it is about devils, the bad ones only, and not unless they do some evil. Otherwise, what would be the use?

It is, however, through this very self-effacement that the Divine together with illusion has slipped into them.

Buddha with the smile that effaces all reality was bound to reign in China. But his Indian gravity has sometimes disappeared.

I visited, among other temples, the temple of the Five Hundred Buddhas, at Canton.

Five hundred. If only there were a single good one in the lot, a really and truly good one! Five hundred, among which was Marco Polo with a hat, probably supplied by the Italian vice-consul. Five hundred, but not one on the road, the very beginning of the road to Holiness.

No more hieratic positions favorable to contemplation. Some hold two or three children in their arms, or play with them. Others, irritated, scratch a thigh, or raise one leg as though in a hurry to go away, waiting with impatience to take a little turn; almost all with the sly little faces of examining magistrates, of examiners, or of eighteenth-century *abbés;* several, obviously, are having a good laugh over the ingenuousness of it all; finally, and these are the most numerous, the careless and evasive Buddhas. 'Oh, you know, we fellows. . . .'

You do not know whether to choke with laughter, with rage, with tears, or simply to think that stronger than the personality of a saint, of a demi-god, is the leveling and vital power of human pettiness.

In a temple, the Chinaman is perfectly at ease. He smokes, he talks, he laughs. At either side of the altar fortune-tellers read the future from ready-printed formulas. Little sticks roll in a box, one always protrudes, and you draw it out. It has a number on it. The leaflet about the future with the corresponding number is found, you read . . . and all you have to do after that is to believe in it.

★

Few Europeans like Chinese music. Yet Confucius, who was not one to exaggerate, far from it, was so much taken with the charm of a melody that he remained three days without being able to eat.

I would not go as far as that, but except for certain Bengalese melodies, I must say it is Chinese music that affects me the most. It moves me. What makes the European so uncomfortable is the orchestra, with its din underlining and interrupting the melody. That is something peculiarly Chinese. Like their fondness for firecrackers and explosives. One has to get used to it. Besides, curiously enough, in spite of this appalling noise, Chinese music is all peace, not sleepy, not slow, but pacific, exempt from the desire to make war, to compel, to command, exempt even from suffering, affectionate.

How good, agreeable and sociable this melody is! It has nothing blaring, idiotic, excited about it, it is quite human and good-natured, childlike and popular, joyful and 'family reunion.'

(With regard to this, the Chinese say that European music is monotonous. 'It is nothing but marches,' they say. Indeed, how the White men do trot and how they blow the trumpet!)

And just as certain people have only to open a book by such-and-such an author and they burst into tears without knowing why, so when I hear a Chinese melody, I feel relieved from the errors and the evil tendencies that are in me and from a kind of excess with which I am afflicted daily.

But there is another charm, not greater, but perhaps more constant; it is the Chinese spoken language.

Compared with this language all others are pedantic, burdened with a thousand ridiculous things, laughable in their monotony—languages for soldiers. That is what they are.

Now the Chinese language was not made like the others, forced by a jostling and controlling syntax. The words in it were not constructed harshly, with authority, method, redundancy, in a conglomeration of resounding syllables, nor along etymological lines. No, just words of one syllable, and that syllable of uncertain resonance. The Chinese sentence resembles weak exclamations. A word rarely contains more than three letters. Often a drowning consonant (the *n* or the *g*) envelops it in the sound of a gong.

Finally, in order to be still closer to nature, this language is sung. There are four tones in the Mandarin language, eight in the dialects of Southern China. None of the monotony of

117

the other languages. With Chinese, one goes up, one goes down, one goes up again, one is halfway there, and one dashes off.

It still remains, it plays with, is completely of, nature.

★

Chinese love is not European love.

The European woman is in a transport of love for you—then all of a sudden she forgets you on the edge of the bed, musing over the serious side of life, about herself, or about nothing, or maybe she has merely relapsed into 'White anxiety.'

The Arab woman behaves like a wave. The stomach dance, do not forget that, is not a mere exhibition for the eyes; no, you are caught in the surge, you are carried away and you find yourself a bit later, blissful, without knowing exactly what has happened to you, nor how.

And she too begins dreaming. Arabia comes between you. All is over.

With the Chinese woman it is not at all like that. The Chinese woman is like the root of the *banyan,* which turns up again everywhere, even among the leaves. Thus she is, and when you have admitted her into your bed, you will not be rid of her for days.

The Chinese woman takes care of you. She considers you are under treatment. Not for a moment does she turn over on her side. Always twined around you, like ivy that does not know how to live alone.

And the most restless man finds her again, near and comfortable like the sheet.

The Chinese woman places herself at your disposal—without cringing, she is not that way, but tactfully and with intelligence.

And she is so affectionate.

A moment comes, following other moments, when almost everyone feels like resting.

You, perhaps; not she. This ant looks immediately for some work to do, and there she is, proceeding to tidy up your valise.

A real lesson in Chinese art. You look at her in amazement. Not a safety pin, not a toothpick does she leave unturned, rearranging them in that perfect order apparently acquired by centuries and centuries of practice and experience.

Every object she becomes familiar with by gestures, trying it, experimenting and judging, and before putting it in place she plays with it. Then, when you see all this in order, the contents of your valise seem now to be rather doll-like, doll-like yet hard, and somehow regulated once for all.

When the Chinese woman talks of love, she can talk indefinitely; she never tires of it; she can even talk about something else, as she often does, she has the language of love, love is made of monosyllables (as soon as a word is lengthened, it looks as if it were going away and taking everything with it; as soon as a sentence appears, the sentence separates you).

The Chinese language is made up of monsyllables, or the shortest, or the most inconsistent ones, and with four singing tones. The singing is discreet. A kind of breeze, or birds' language. A language so moderate and affectionate that one could hear it all one's life without getting bored, even when not understanding it.

Such is the Chinese woman. And yet, all that would be nothing did she not answer to the admirable definition of the word 'mitschlafen,' to sleep with. There are men who are so

119

restless that they even throw their pillows on the ground without realizing it.

What does the Chinese woman do? I do not know; a sort of sense of harmony, subsisting in her sleep, enables her, by appropriate movements, to remain attached, always to subordinate herself to what, all the same, would be so wonderful—to be harmoniously two.

In Europe everything ends tragically. There has never been any philosophy in Europe (at least since the Greeks . . . and even with them it is questionable).

The French with their social tragedy, the Greeks with their Oedipus, the Russians with their love of misfortune, the Italians with their pride in tragedy, the Spanish with their tragic obsession, Hamletism, etc., etc.

If Christ had not been crucified, he would not have had a hundred disciples in Europe.

His *Passion* is what excited people.

What would the Spaniards do if they did not see the wounds of Christ? And all European literature is about suffering, never about wisdom. One has to wait for the American Walt Whitman and the author of *Walden* to hear another note.

Therefore, that of the Chinese, which is almost devoid of heartbreak poetry, of complaint, has no charm whatsoever for the European, excepting a hundred or so librarians, who by dint of reading know nothing whatsoever about anything.

The Chinese sees nothing tragic at all in death. A Chinese

philosopher declares very simply: 'An old man who does not know how to die I call a good-for-nothing.' There you have it.

In fact, one-third of China is a cemetery. But what a cemetery!

The Chinese country, when I saw it for the first time, went right to my heart. Tombs, whole mountains (or rather the side of one, the eastern slope of another) covered with tombs, but not hard, straight tombs, no—semicircles of stones . . . that are inviting. Unmistakably, they are inviting. Indeed, they do not frighten anyone. Every Chinaman has his coffin while he is alive. He is quite at ease with death.

When a man dies in a distant province, a room is made ready, while waiting to find a way to transport him back to his country—a room where the members of the family, the son, the daughter, etc., come from time to time, to meet, to meditate a little, to eat, talk and play majong.

★

The *paintings,* the *theater,* and *Chinese handwriting,* more than anything else, show this extreme reserve, this inner concavity, this lack of *aura* of which I spoke. Chinese paintings are mainly landscapes. The movement of things is indicated, not their thickness and their weight, but their linearness, if one may say so. The Chinaman possesses the faculty of reducing the being to what signifies the being (somewhat like the mathematical or algebraic faculty). If a combat is to take place, he does not go into combat, he does not even pretend to do so. He signifies it. That is all that interests him; the combat itself would seem coarse to him. And this signification is established by something so slight that a simple European cannot hope to decipher the piece. All the more so as there are

121

hundreds of them. In addition to that, a quantity of elements are taken apart and then put together again in fragments, as one would do in algebra.

If the subject is a flight, everything will be represented except the flight—the sweat, the glances to right and left, but not the flight. If they show you old age, you will have it all there, except the look of old age, and the gait of old age; but you will have, for example, the beard and the lame knee.

In the creating of Chinese characters, this lack of a gift for mass effects, and for the spontaneous, and this taste for taking a detail to signify the whole is more striking still, and it is why Chinese, which might have been a universal language, has never, except in the case of Korea and of Japan, crossed the Chinese frontier—and moreover is supposed to be the most difficult of the languages.

The trouble is that there are not five characters in the twenty thousand that one can guess at first glance. Not a hundred simple characters even in the primitive writing. The Chinaman wants general effects.

Let us take something that should be quite easy to represent: a chair. It is formed by the following characters (they themselves unrecognizable):

1) tree; 2) tall; 3) to sigh with pleasure, in admiration: the whole makes *chair,* and is recomposed, no doubt, as follows: *man* (sitting on his heels or standing up). *Sighing with pleasure near an object made of the wood of a tree.* And if one only saw the different elements! But if one does not know them in advance, one will not discover them.

The idea of representing the chair itself with its seat and its legs does not occur to him.

But the chair that suited him he has found; not obvious but discreet, pleasantly suggested by elements of the landscape, deduced by the mind rather than designated, and yet uncertain and as though 'played at.'

This character, which is one of the easiest of the composed characters, shows plainly enough how repugnant it is to a Chinaman to see an object as it is, and on the other hand, the delight he takes in general effects, in the landscape with figures. Even if the Chinaman represents an object as it is, in no time he reshapes and simplifies it. Example: The elephant, during the centuries, has taken eight forms.*

In the first place, it had a trunk. A few centuries later, it has it still. But the animal has been made to stand up like a man. Some time later, it loses its eye and its head, after that its body, keeping only its feet, its spinal column and its shoulders. Then it recovers its head, loses the rest, except the feet, then writhes in the form of a serpent. To finish up, it is anything you like; it has two horns and a nipple that comes out of one foot.

★

Chinese poetry is so very delicate that it never meets an *idea* (in the European sense of the word).

A Chinese poem cannot be translated. Neither in painting, nor in poetry, nor in the drama, has the Chinese that warm, thick voluptuousness of the Europeans. In a poem, he indicates, and the points indicated are not even the most important ones, their evidence is not hallucinating, they are avoided, they are not even suggested, as it is often said, but rather the landscape and its atmosphere are deduced from them.

When Li Po says to us such apparently easy things as this, and it is one third of the poem:

* *'The Evolution of Chinese Writing,' Owen. p. 8, fig. I.*

Blue is the water and clear the moon of autumn.
We pluck white lilies in the South lake.
They seem to sigh with love
filling with melancholy the heart of the man in the boat.

It must be said, in the first place, that the painter's eye is so prevalent in China that with no other indication the reader sees this in a satisfying manner, enjoys it, and quite naturally can draw a picture of it for you with a brush. Of this faculty, an ancient example:

Toward the sixteenth century, I do not know under what emperor, the Chinese police had made by stealth, by their inspectors, the portrait of every foreigner coming into China. Ten years after having seen only the portrait, a member of the police recognized you. Better still, if a crime was committed and the assassin had disappeared, there was always someone in the neighborhood who could do *from memory* the portrait of the assassin, which, reproduced in several copies, was sent off at breakneck speed over the great highways of the Empire. Hemmed in on all sides by his portraits, the assassin was obliged to give himself up to the judge.

In spite of this gift for seeing, a Chinaman would have little interest in a French or English translation of the poem.

After all, what do these four lines of Li Po contain in French? A scene.

But in Chinese, they contain thirty or so; it is a bazaar, it is a cinema, it is a great picture. Each word is a landscape, a group of signs, the elements of which, even in the briefest poem, combine with endless allusions. A Chinese poem is always too long, such is its superabundance, but it really excites one, it is bristling with comparisons.

In the *'blue'* ("Spirit of Chinese Poetry," by V. W. W. S. Purcell), there is the sign of chopping wood and that of water, not to mention silk. In *bright,* there is the moon, and at the same time the sun. In *autumn,* you have fire, and corn, and so on.

The fact is that three lines suffice to give such an affluence of parallels and of fine points that one's delight is intense.

This delight is obtained by *equilibrium and harmony,* a state pleasing beyond all else to the Chinaman, for whom it is a kind of *paradise.**

This sentiment, even more opposed to the exalted Hindu peace than to the restlessness and action of the European, is to be found nowhere but among the yellow races.

★

What the Chinaman knows best is the art of escaping.

A profoundly 'Pilate' people. In the street you ask a Chinaman for information, and immediately he runs off. *'It's wiser,'* he thinks, *'not to mix in other people's business. One begins by giving information, and ends in blows.'*

People who run away at the slightest provocation and whose little eyes scoot over to the corners when you look them in the face.

A Chinese general who does it in his trousers, who begs the colonel to take his place in the battle, surprises no one. No one asks to see his trousers. Everybody thinks this quite natural.**

* *The Chinese has always wanted* UNIVERSAL AGREEMENT *where heaven and earth* MAY BE IN A STATE OF PERFECT SERENITY *and where all beings* REACH THEIR COMPLETE DEVELOPMENT.
A man who was plotting to stir up the people said: 'The Emperor is no longer IN HARMONY WITH HEAVEN.' *At these words, the peasants, horror-stricken, and the nobility and everybody, rushed to take arms . . . and the Emperor lost his throne.*
** *In war, he follows readily the precept:* 'Hesitating whether to advance one inch, I prefer to retreat one step.'

One day I saw five officers who were swearing to exterminate I don't remember whom. They looked like rabbits (and yet the Chinese were and are once more becoming the best soldiers in the world).

An old, old childish people that does not want to know what is at the bottom of anything, that has no principles, but 'cases'; no law, but 'cases'; no morale, but 'cases.'

The lie, so-called, does not exist in China.

The lie is the creation of excessively upright minds, militarily upright, just as immodesty is an invention of people far removed from nature.

The Chinaman adapts himself, barters, calculates, exchanges.

He goes with the crowd. The Chinese peasant believes that he has *three hundred souls*.*

Everything that is tortuous in nature is to him a gentle caress.

He considers the root more 'nature' than the trunk.

If he finds a big stone, with holes in it, or cracked, he takes it in as his child, or rather as his father, and places it on a pedestal in his garden.

When you perceive at twenty yards in front of you a monument or a house, do not imagine that you will be nearer to it in a few seconds. Nothing is straight, infinite turnings lead to it and perhaps you will lose your way, and never reach what was right in front of your nose.

This is to throw the 'demons' off the track, as they can only walk in a straight line, but above all because everything that is straight makes the Chinaman ill-at-ease and gives him the painful impression of error.

Morale of a drugged anemic people.

* *'The Chinese Idea of the Second Self,' by E. T. C. Werner.*

126

(Is it by chance that the women all have the look of vicious boarding-school girls with their hair cut across the forehead?)

Philosophy for little children. 'Say a nice "thank you." Bow, take off your hat, don't pass in front of the others. Don't scream. Don't take up the middle of the street. Think of your future, of your parents. Don't pinch your comrades, etc.'

'If you go out with one who is your superior, apply rule 72 in the manual; with a professor, rule 18, for going home, rule No. 44; then apply ritual C and, if a Mandarin is making a visit with bonnet B4, salute him with ceremonial 422, repeating words 4007.'

Thus he will not *lose face*. From the lowest coolie up to the highest mandarin, the thing is not to lose face, their wooden face, but they do care about it and, in fact, having no principles, it is the face that counts.

Wisdom of little tots, but one that has amazing and unexpected advantages over other civilizations, due, no doubt, to the Chinaman's sense of the *efficacious* (he is the inventor of jiu-jitsu).

Courtesy, gentleness, are, eight hundred years before Confucius, indicated as essential qualities in the 'historic books.'

★

To obey wisdom, a reasonable politico-shopkeeping wisdom, discussed and practical, has always been a matter of concern to the Chinese.

The Chinese have always demanded wisdom on the part of their emperors. Their philosophers spoke to them as those who have the upper hand speak. The emperor was in fear of having *to blush* . . . before them.

The bandit evades the laws of the empire, but not that law.

A thoughtless bandit would never succeed in enrolling a single man.

On the contrary, the wise bandit gets a great deal of support.

In China, nothing is absolute. No principle, no *a priori*. And nothing shocks the victim. The bandit is considered as an element of natural force.

This element is one of those with which small transactions are made. One does not suppress it, one arranges with it. One deals with it.

It is practically impossible, in China, to go outside of a city; twenty minutes away from it, they catch you. However, in the heart of China perhaps you will not get caught. But nowhere does security exist. There are pirates two hours from Macao, two hours from Hong Kong, who seize boats.

Now the Chinese, the Chinese businessman, is the first to fall a victim to them.

Never mind. For the Chinaman to see clearly, things must first be complicated. So that he may see clearly at home, he must have at least ten children and a concubine. So that he may see clearly in the streets, they must be labyrinths. So that the city may be gay, he must have a country fair.

So that he may go to the theater, it must have, in the same building, *eight to ten theaters* for dramas, comedies, films, plus a gallery for prostitutes, accompanied by their mothers, a few games of skill and of chance, and, in one corner, a lion and a panther.

A Chinese shopping street is stuffed with signs and advertisements. They hang from every side. You do not know what to look at.

How empty is the European city* beside this; empty, clean, yes! and earthy.

So that he may feel fit, the Chinaman must have on his body the dirt of ninety days.

★

The Chinaman is neither honest nor dishonest.

If it is the time to be honest, he will take up honesty as one would take up a language.

When, in doing business with Englishmen, you have been conducting your correspondence in English, *all* your letters will be in English, and not all less five or six a month; thus, the Chinaman who takes up honesty of the rigid type is perfectly honest. He does not swerve from the rigid type; he is more faithful than the European.

But honest though he may be, dishonesty does not shock him. In fact, there is no dishonesty in nature. Is a caterpillar that eats the leaf of a cherry tree dishonest? And yet the Chinaman, before the arrival of the European, was famous throughout Asia for his remarkable honesty in business matters.

★

Europeans (Germanic, Gauls, Anglo-Saxons) out-Chinese the Chinese. It is often said that the Chinese invented everything . . . ahem!

It is believed that the Chinese swarm because they have a great many children. Not at all; they have a great many children because they like to swarm . . . and to occupy space. They like the general effect, not the individual; the panorama, not the single object.

129

Curiously enough, it is precisely the Europeans who have re-invented and 're-searched' what the Chinese have invented and researched.

When the Chinese boast of having discovered diabolo, polo, football, archery, jiu-jitsu, paper, etc.—well, what is one to do about it? That does not prove that the Chinese is superior. It is does not prove that the European is superior either. It proves the superiority of the Hindu who, intensely cultivated, did not invent diabolo, football, etc.

Were I a civilization, I would not boast of having invented diabolo. No indeed; instead of that I would be ashamed of it, and I would hide from myself. I would make better resolutions for the future.

The Chinese and the Whites suffer from the same malady.

During the day they potter, then they have to play games.

Without their theater, the Chinese in the cities would find life insupportable. They need a thousand games.

Playing games, he is alive. At Macao, in the gambling dens, they become slightly animated; but fearing ridicule, they soon go out to take a pipe of opium and, having regained their wooden countenance, they return to the room.

Every instant, in the street, one hears pennies falling, and shouts of 'heads or tail,' and immediately a group of anxious faces, watching and praying.

In spite of all these games, a malady awaits the Chinaman: he finds himself unable to laugh any more. What with dissembling, making plans, composing his face, he no longer knows how to laugh. Terrible malady. There was a devoted child who, for filial love, stumbled and fell over some buckets of water to divert his parents afflicted with 'the malady.' Now when one knows how the Chinaman: 1) has a horror of water; 2) fears ridicule, one realizes the seriousness of the malady that must be cured, and the tremendous duties of filial love in China.

★

Chinamen should always be thought of as animals. The Hindus, as other animals, the Japanese ditto, and the Russians and the Germans, and so on. And in each race these three varities: the adult man, the child, and the woman. Three worlds. A man is a creature who understands nothing about a child, and nothing about a woman.

And neither they nor ourselves are right. We are obviously wrong, all of us.

Also, the question of whether Confucius is a great man need not be raised. The question is to know whether he was a great Chinaman, and thoroughly understood the Chinese, which seems to be true, and directed them for the best, which is not so certain.

Ditto Buddha for India, etc., etc.

In these different human species, their philosophy generally approaches the type or the race, but occasionally it is remote from it.

That is why it is difficult to know how far Confucius and Lao-Tsu have Chinesed the Chinese, or have un-Chinesed them, or how far Mencius, placing the Empire's ban on war and the military, has fostered Chinese cowardice or affected the combativeness of the Chinese. It must be remembered that the Chinaman who runs amok is a demon that nothing can stop, and compared to whom a Malay is quite gentle, and that acts of courage were at least as abundant in China as elsewhere, and that their indifference to death and privation is incomparable.

The Chinese are not mere dreamers. They have not had transcendental systems or strokes of genius, but they made discoveries of incalculable practical value.

Confucius: the Edison of morality.

Kindliness, calm (do not meddle with what does not concern you. Behave according to your condition; if you are powerful, like a powerful person, if you are head over ears in debt, like a man head over ears in debt, etc.), correctness in attire, politeness. . . .

No one has concerned himself with the relations between human beings with as much solicitude and foresight as the Chinese.

Sun Yat Sen said very justly: 'Where politics are concerned, China has nothing to learn from Europe.' In fact, she might give lessons to Europe and even India in the art—having done everything, put everything into practice, including the systematic absence of government.

Without municipality, without lawyers (if one of them turns up, he is put in prison . . . lawyers attract trials), without armies (armies attract wars), she has been able to live very well for quite a time, all the time that the Chinese were sufficiently wise.

When you are no longer wise, then, alas, you must have strong administrations. But nothing prevents or could prevent wars, revolution and destruction (see Europe, nineteenth century).

The Chinaman does not insist on his duty toward humanity in general, but toward *his* father and *his* mother; it is where one lives that things must go smoothly and that requires a touch and a virtue such as a European saint would be scarcely capable of showing.

★

The romantic Chinaman is as yet unborn. He always wants *to look* reasonable.

Tsin che Hoang Ti is one of the most famous and fantastic tyrants in the world, who had a whole mountain painted red (color of the condemned) because his people had got caught in a storm on it.

Tsin che Hoang Ti, who had a bath of boiling water prepared in the Throne-room when one of his officers demanded an audience which displeased him, was the same emperor who had engraved stone tablets all over the place reading: 'All is well. Weights and measures are standardized. Men are good husbands, parents are respected!

'Wherever the wind blows, everybody is glad,' etc.

On the other hand, in a theatrical piece, no matter what its subject every five minutes there is a scene where they take council. One would think oneself at a trial. And the actors come in saying: 'I am so and so, I come from . . ., I am going to . . .,' in order that there may be no confusion. To explain carefully, that is reasonable.

★

The Chinese detest us as cursed meddlers, who cannot keep our hands off anything. Ammunition, tinned food, missionaries, we have to throw our activities at their heads.

And so, what hatred, and, in the Extreme Orient, what

jealousy too! And how can one appear innocent? But from having seen this hatred constantly turned on me, I was affected perhaps by it myself, in my attitude to them.

★

The Chinaman has the love of imitation carried to such a degree, submits himself so naturally to the model, that one is ill at ease.*

This mania is so rooted in them that the Chinese philosophers have based almost their whole morality upon it, which is a morality of *example.*

The book of verses says:

'The Prince, whose conduct is always full of equity and of wisdom, will see men from the four parts of the world imitate his uprightness. He accomplishes his duty as a father, as a son, as an elder brother, and as a younger brother and *then people imitate him.'*

There you are, you have done the trick! It is irresistible. Now everything is going to go like clockwork.

The Chinaman must have been amazed to see the European not imitating him. That is: he had a chance to be amazed. But a Chinaman would die rather than be amazed.

The current idea among Chinese art critics is that paintings *must take the place of nature,* that pictures should convey such a strong impression of it that the city-dweller need no

* *He copies without a single mistake and with no previous experience a Paris gown. The Museum in Pekin contains thousands of plants made of stone, in various colours, pots of flowers, imitations that one can hardly detect. The Chinaman prefers them to natural flowers. He also copies shells and stones. He copies lava in bronze. He places in his garden* ARTIFICIAL CINDERS MADE OF CONCRETE.

134

longer take the trouble to go to the country, which, in fact, is what happens.

The *sampans,* on the river at Canton, are desperately bare, but there are always one or two pictures hung up inside.

In the worst Chinese hovels one sees pictures with wide horizons, with superb mountains.

★

An ancient Chinese philosopher, to encourage virtue, makes the following rather silly pronouncement, 'that if the government of a small state is good, everyone (everyone who is Chinese, of course) will flock to it,' and its power and prosperity will be augmented.

He knew his Chinese people, wise old Chinaman that he was.

The thing can still be verified today. Malaya has a stable and reliable government. The Chinese flock to it. There are two millions of them there. Singapore is a Chinese city. Malaya, a friend was saying to me, is a Chinese colony administered by the English.

Javanese trade is in the hands of the Chinese. In the tiniest villages, they have their shop.

In Borneo, or even in Bali, where the inhabitants keep to themselves and do not need anyone, some Chinese have managed to install themselves and to do business.

They tell us that Confucius and his disciples one day met a woman (I give you the story roughly). . . . They learn that her father has been swept away by a flood, her husband killed by a tiger, her brother bitten by a snake, and one of her sons involved in a misfortune of much the same type.

Then Confucius, disconcerted, says: 'And you remain in a country such as this?' (It was a small state in China that she could easily have left to go to another one.)

The woman then gives this charmingly Chinese reply: 'The government here is not too bad!'

That is to say, in good English, that business was going well, that taxes were moderate.

Things like that root you to the spot. Confucius himself was wide-eyed when he heard it.

★

Do the Chinese ever see things on a large scale?

They are particularly good workers on little tasks.

They have been able to appear profound in politics on account of their pleasant principle of 'Let it alone, everything will come out all right,' which they keep for great matters.

But one notices that they go on exactly the opposite principle where smaller matters are concerned, leaving no stone unturned in order to succeed in arranging their own affairs, small or large, more often small.

They make plans, mark boundaries, arrange things in such a way as to have something to fall back on, set traps, and have always acted thus, because they have always liked to contrive.

Every creature is born with an idea, a principle that does not need to be proved, is generally far from being transcendental, and around which he assembles his notions. . . . It is generally believed that the central, intimate idea of Confucius was one's obligations to the family, to the prince and to wisdom. What do we know about it?

An idea, too essential, too intimate for him, for the Chinese to perceive, was used as a base by him constantly. It was perhaps that man was made for bargaining.*

In the eighteenth century, a great Chinese author was racking his brains. He wanted an absolutely fantastic tale, breaking the laws of the world. What did he find? This: His hero, a sort of Gulliver, arrives in a country where the *merchants were trying to sell things at ridiculously low prices, and where the customers were insisting on paying exorbitant prices.* After that, the author believed he had shaken the foundations of the universe and of all the planets.** Nothing so strange, thinks this Chinaman, exists anywhere in the world.

Among the characteristics common to all the peoples of the yellow races is their addiction to intoxicants.

One is apt to believe that it is opium that has done the harm, and that it might have been as well not to have the poppy in China to supply the opium, and consequently . . .

Opium has nothing to do with it.

Fifteen centuries ago the Chinese did not smoke. He was only a drunkard. He drank wine and rice alcohol.

* *The Chinaman can negotiate anything: an insult, an army, a city, a sentiment and even his death. He trades his conversion for a watch, and his death for a coffin (for a good wooden coffin, coolies have been known to have themselves executed in the place of condemned persons richer than they). To the first Portuguese Catholics, eager to convert the heathen, the Chinese offered to trade twelve hundred baptisms for a cannon. A good mortar was worth three thousand of them.*

** *I notice with Giles that Herbert Spencer had thought of this, exactly this. Yet a philosopher. But the philosopher of a nation of shopkeepers is more profoundly shopkeeper than philosopher, just as a hunting dog is not so much hunting dog as he is dog.*

137

Opium does not suffice with the Chinaman. He smokes tobacco. The women smoke. In the shops, in the street, and they throw away a cigarette only to take another one. Without a cigarette, obviously, they could not choose a stuff.

Japan is full of drunkards. They zigzag everywhere in the street.

The Burmese, at the age of four, smoke already, little girls as well as little boys, and not cigarettes, but big, dirty, strong cigars, 'cheroots.'

The Indo-Chinese take opium.

The Koreans take opium and morphine.

The Chinese and the Japanese are fond of toys, of the artificial, of well-being, of lanterns, of artificial lighting, of dwarf or cardboard trees. They are nocturnal. Their cities are alive at night.

He has the peace that goes with drugs. Enjoys being without any motion, except when it's hysterical, and likes to hear shrill sounds.

The Chinaman is not very sensual, yet at the same time he is very much so. But finely.

He has, so to speak, no ancient erotic literature. He is not disturbed by a woman, nor is a woman by a man. He is not even disturbed at the moment when everyone is disturbed. That is of no consequence. That leaves no trace. No, that does not stir his blood. Everything takes place in a springtime, fresh and still near to winter. If he has really a desire, it will be for a little girl still retaining the line of childhood, delicate and thin. He is not dirty. Obscene Chinese postcards are extremely witty. His music always has a transparent quality. He does not understand the heavy voluptuousness of the European, that warm thick tone of European voices, musical instruments and tales does not exist for him, he has none of the sickening sentimentality of the English or American, French or Viennese, that feeling of the long kiss, of stickiness, and of the submerging of self.

A Chinese prostitute is less obviously sensual than a European mother of a family. She immediately shows affection. She seeks to attach herself.

Chinese painting is cleanliness, absence of impressionism, of excitement. There is no air between the objects, nothing but pure ether. The objects are traced; they seem to be memories. It is they, and yet they are absent, like delicate phantoms that desire has not raised. The Chinaman likes distant horizons above everything . . . things that cannot be touched.

The European wants to be able to touch. The air in his pictures is thick. His nudes are almost lewd, even when the subject is taken from the Bible. Passion, desire, hands maul them.

The Chinaman has a genius for the sign. Beside Chinese writing, Egyptian writing is bestial, it is particularly stupid. The most ancient Chinese writing, that to be found on seals, was already free from voluptuousness in its presentation and tracing, almost so in its symbols; the writing that succeeded it lost its circles, curves and all envelopments. Freed from imitation, it became quite cerebral, thin and 'un-enveloping' (to envelop: voluptuousness).

And only the Chinese theater is a theater for the mind.

Only the Chinese know what a theatrical production is. The Europeans have, for a long time, produced nothing at all. The Europeans show you everything. Everything is there, on the stage. Every object, nothing is missing, not even the view from the window.

The Chinese, on the contrary, who is a simple creature, and marvelously clever, brings out whatever is needed to indicate a landscape, or trees, or a ladder, according to what is required. As the scene changes every three minutes, there would be no end to the installing of furniture, of objects, etc. His theater is extremely rapid, like a cinema.

He can show a great many more objects and outdoor scenes than we can.

The music indicates the type of action or of sentiment, and even a European is finally able to follow.

Each actor comes on the scene with a costume and a face painted in such a way that it tells you at once who he is. Impossible to cheat. He can say anything he likes. We know what we know.

His character is painted on his face. Red if he is brave, white with a black stripe if he is a traitor, and we know exactly to what degree; if he has only a bit of white on his nose, he is a figure of fun, etc.

If he needs great space, he simply looks off into the distance; and who would look off into the distance if there were no horizon? When a woman has to sew a dress, she at once begins to sew. Only the pure air shifts between her fingers, nevertheless everyone feels the sensation of sewing, of the needle (for who would sew pure air?) going in, and coming out with difficulty on the other side; and one's impression is even stronger than in reality; one feels the cold and everything. Why? Because the actor pictures the thing to himself. A sort of magnetism makes its appearance with him, coming from his desire to feel what is absent.

When you see him pour, with the greatest care, from a non-existent jug, non-existent water onto a non-existent cloth and rub his face with it, and wring out the non-existent cloth just as it should be done, the existence of this water, unapparent and yet evident, becomes somehow hallucinating, and if the actor lets the jug fall (non-existent) and you are in the front row, you feel you have been splashed like he has.

There are plays where the action is terrific, where non-existent walls are scaled, with the aid of non-existent ladders, in order to steal non-existent money chests.

There are often, in comic plays, twenty minutes or more of almost uninterrupted miming.

The miming language of lovers is something exquisite; it is better than words, more tangible, more imperious, more spontaneous, and central; it is fresher than love, less exaggerated than dancing, less domestic; and what is really remarkable, one can represent *everything* without its being shocking.

I saw, for example, a prince who was traveling incognito ask a servant-girl at the inn, by gestures, if he could sleep with her.

She replied, in the same manner, by a lot of impossibilities.

Sleeping proposals always seem difficult to separate from a certain sensuality. Well, it is curious, but there was none. Not a sign of it, and it lasted for at least a quarter of an hour. It became an obsession with this little young man. The whole house was amused. But never did that obsession become embarrassing. She was not *in flesh,* but had got as far as being outlined like certain faces seen in a dream, free from any vulgarity.

★

Chinese style, particularly the very ancient style of the Mings, of the Six dynasties, of the Tangs, is extraordinary. No lyrical development, no unilinear progression.

Suddenly your are stopped, you can go no further. Old

Chinese stories always seem disconnected. They have stumps. They are chopped off. Compared to them one of our stories looks as if it were full of tricks; and in fact the richest grammar, the most mobile phrase, is nothing but sleight-of-hand with the elements of thought.

The thought, the phrase of the Chinese is right before you. And it stands solidly, like a chest, and if the phrases flow and are linked, it is the translator who has made them flow.

A grandeur like that from a pot of stew emanates from it.

Lao-Tsu, Chuang-Tsu in their philosophy, Kao-Ti (the peasant who became emperor) in his proclamations to the Chinese, Wu-Ti in his letter to the captain of the Huns, have this extraordinary style. A style that economizes words.

★

Nothing approaches the style of Lao-Tsu. Lao-Tsu throws you a big pebble. Then he goes away. After that he throws you another pebble, then goes away again; all his pebbles, though very hard, are fruit, but naturally the old bear is not going to peel them for you.

★

Lao-Tsu is a man who knows. He touches bottom. He speaks the language of evidence. He says nothing that is not clear, certain. Nevertheless, he is not understood. 'The *Tao* that is expressed in words is not the true *Tao*. How small! How great! How unfathomable! . . . —What does the water of rivers do to reign over the torrents of the high mountains and the streams?

'—It knows how to keep to a lower level.

142

'Work by inaction.

'With inaction everything is possible. . . .

'Annihilate one's being and one's action, and the universe comes to you.'

His Taoist disciples cultivated all this for magic, rather than for moral purposes.

A man thus effaced is no longer struck by substances, nor by phenomena.

A hunter, to frighten the game, set the forest on fire. Suddenly he saw a man who was coming out of a rock. This man then went through the fire deliberately.

The hunter ran after him.

—Heigh, tell me. How do you manage to pass through the rock?

—The rock? What do you mean by that?

—And you have been seen to pass through the fire as well.

—The fire? What do you mean by the fire?

This Taoist, perfect, completely effaced, no longer noticed any difference in anything.

At other times he lived among lions, and the lions did not realize that he was a man. They noticed nothing strange about him.

Such is the pliability that the understanding of *Tao* gives one. Such is the supreme effacement of which so many Chinese have dreamed.

★

The Chinaman is not particularly dashing. A Chinese city is conspicuous for its formidable gates. What one needs first of all is to be protected. Rather than too many proud monuments in the interior, imposing gates, strongly built, for the purpose of frightening people away, but for us, so obviously a bluff.

The Chinese empire is distinguishable among all others for its Wall of China. What one needs first of all is to be protected.

Chinese edifices are distinguishable for their roofs. What one needs first of all is to be protected.

Everywhere there are great screens, then there are again smaller ones, and naturally triple labyrinths. What is needed first of all is proper protection.

The Chinaman never lets himself go, but is always on his guard; he always has the air of belonging to a secret society.

Though warlike when it was absolutely necessary, China was always a peace-loving nation. *'With good steel, one does not make nails. Of a young man of worth, do not make a soldier.'* Such is public opinion. All Chinese education lays so much stress on pacifism that the Chinese had become cowards (for a time), and most unblushingly.*

The Chinaman, who can carve splendid and sedate camels, as well as horses, with a great deal of humor, has not been able to render the lion. His lions make grimaces, but they are not lions. They are more like eunuchs.

Natural ardor, hot blood and natural aggressiveness, the Chinaman is unable to grasp.

China is so essentially peaceful that it is full of bandits. If the Chinese people were not so peace-loving, they would take arms at all costs and restore order. However, they would rather not.

The peasant, the small tradesman, finds himself ruined, plundered, or even ten times plundered. Yet after the tenth time he still has a little patience left in reserve.

* *When put to the test, they again became invincible soldiers.*

144

The Chinaman lives comfortably in the midst of this insecurity in the interior of China, where you risk your property and your life, and which is so insupportable and distressing to the European. As a player of games, he knows how to behave as a toy.

★

It is in Pekin that I understood the willow, not the weeping willow, but the straight willow, the Chinese tree *par excellence*.

The willow has something evasive about it. Its foliage is impalpable, its movement resembles a meeting of breezes. There is more of it than one sees, more than it shows of itself. It is the least ostentatious of trees. And though always shivering (not the brief and anxious shiver of the birches and of the poplars), it does not look as if it were contained in itself, nor attached, but always sailing and swimming so as to maintain its place in the wind, like fish in the river's current.

It is little by little that the willow educates you, giving you its lesson each morning. And a repose made of vibration seizes you, so that when it ends, you can no longer open the window without feeling a desire to weep.

★

In things that seem at first to be almost neutral, but which are immediately revealed to him (to us after a while) with a heartrending mystic sweetness, the Chinaman has placed his infinite—a just and enjoyable infinite.

Jade, polished stones that seem moist but not shiny, clouded and not transparent, ivory, the moon, a single flower

145

in its flower pot, little branches with their multiple twigs, their tiny leaves; thin, vibrating, far-off landscapes caught in a rising mist, stones pierced and as though tortured, a woman's song heard faintly in the distance, plants under water, the lotus, the short, flutelike whistle of the toad in the silence, flavorless dishes, a slightly decayed egg, gummy macaroni, a shark's fin, a light rain falling, a son who accomplishes the acts of filial piety and follows the rites in too exact a manner—so strained, this exactitude, it makes you faint—imitation in all its forms, plants made of stone, creamy flowers with corollas, petals and sepals of an irritating perfection; to have theatrical performances at court, played by political prisoners, obliging them to do it; delicious, half absent-minded cruelties—here is what the Chinese has always liked.

★

The Chinaman, among all the peoples of the yellow race, has something about him that is powerful, and particularly that is heavy—he himself somewhat barrel-shaped with his cylindrical forms, when he begins to get on in years.

Beside the great *Chien Meng* gate at Pekin, the *Arc de Triomphe* seems light and removable. A Chinese bathtub in the South is often a great earthen pot (from which water is dipped by little jugfuls that one throws on one's body), that is all, a great pot, oh, how heavy! and it seems as if it would be easier to move a grand piano about. The Chinaman gives the impression of something squatting. His sculptured lions are like toads that grimace. His bronze cranes, his geese weigh on the ground like men, human birds that have ceased to count on anything but the solid earth. His furniture is stocky. His lanterns large and big-bellied, and every house has two or

146

three of these barrels suspended in the air that slowly oscillate.

In miserable, absolutely bare interiors sometimes there is a great red ewer, like a patriarch enthroned.

The Chinese characters on Japanese posters are thin, drawn with fine strokes. On the Chinese posters, the characters are pot-bellied, real tumblers, like a hippopotamus' bottom, and stand crushed down one on top of another, with a burlesque, heavy self-assurance, like the gravest and the most disturbing notes of the double-bass.

No city has gates as massive as those of Pekin.

★

You must really get it into your head that the Chinaman is a most sensitive creature. He has kept the heart of a youngster. For four thousand years he has kept the heart of a youngster.

Is it a good child? Not especially. But he is impressionable, is the Chinaman, a trembling leaf makes his heart rock, a fish sailing slowly by makes him almost swoon. He who has not heard Mei-Lan-Fang does not know what gentleness is, heartrending gentleness, decomposing, the liking for tears, the painful refinement of grace.

And even a textbook on painting, such as that of Wang-Wei, or the one by Ly-Yu, entitled *The Garden of the Mustard-seed,* is done so devoutly and so movingly that it makes the tears come into one's eyes.

A trifle hurts the Chinaman's feelings.

A youngster is terribly afraid of humiliations.

Who has not felt himself to be *Poil de Carotte?* The fear of humiliations is so Chinese that it dominates their civilization. They are polite for that reason. To avoid humiliating the other. They humiliate themselves to avoid being humiliated.

Politeness, that is a way to prevent humiliation. They smile.

They are not so much afraid of losing face as of making others lose it. This sensitiveness, really unhealthy from the European viewpoint, gives a particular aspect to their whole civilization. They have the sense and the apprehension of 'people are saying.' They always feel they are being observed. . . . 'When thou goest through an orchard, take care, if there are apples, to put thy hand to thy trousers, and if there are melons, to touch thy boots.' They are not conscious of themselves, but of their appearance, as though they themselves were on the outside and observing themselves from there. From the earliest days this order existed in the Chinese army: 'And now look fierce!'

Even the emperors, when there were emperors, were afraid of being humiliated. Speaking of Barbarians, of Koreans, they said to their messenger: Arrange so that they do *not laugh* at us. —To be the laughing-stock. The Chinese are offended more easily than anyone and their literature contains, as one might expect on the part of men who are polite and easily hurt, the most cruel and infernal insolence.

★

Is the change in me due to China? I always had a weakness for the tiger. When I saw one, it stirred up something in me, and at once I was one with it.

But yesterday I was at the *Great World*. I saw a tiger that was near the entrance (a fine tiger), and I perceived that it was a stranger to me. I perceived that the tiger has the head of an idiot, passionate and monomaniacal. But the roads that each creature follows are so little known that the tiger might all the same arrive at wisdom. One sees, in fact, that he has the air of being perfectly at ease.

★

Today, perhaps for the thousandth time in my life, I watched children playing (white people's). The first pleasure the child has in the exercise of his intelligence is not derived from his judgment nor from his memory.

No, it is from ideography.

They put a board on the ground, and that board becomes a ship, they agree that it is a ship; they lay a smaller one beside it, which becomes a gangway, or bridge.

And then (what is still more curious, several of them agree), an irregular and fortuitous line of light and shade becomes the shore, and maneuvering according to their signs, embarking, disembarking, standing out to sea, while none but the enlightened would guess what it was all about: that this is a ship, here the bridge, that the bridge is raised . . . and all the complications (and these are innumerable) in which they are involved as they go along.

But the suggestion is there, evident to those who have accepted it, and it is the suggestion, and not the thing, that delights them.

The ease with which it is manipulated appeals to their intelligence, for the actual things are much more awkward to handle. In the present case, it was a complete demonstration. Those children were playing on the deck of a ship.

It is curious that this pleasure in suggestions was for centuries the great pleasure of the Chinese and the very kernel of their mental and general development.

A BARBARIAN

IN JAPAN

"It is because we are in Paradise that everything in this world hurts us. Outside of Paradise, nothing embarrasses for nothing matters."

I should like to find myself excused by these charming words of Komachi, the Japanese poetess, for having had unfavorable impressions of Japan.

What the Japanese lack is a great river. 'Wisdom accompanies rivers,' says a Chinese proverb. Wisdom and peace. They have nothing in the way of peace, but instead a volcano, a majestic mountain, no doubt, but none the less a volcano, that inundates them regularly with mud, lava and disasters.

Not only is a great river lacking, but tall trees and wide spaces. I covered twelve hundred kilometers in vaunted provinces of Japan without seeing any fine trees. I know very well that fine landscapes rarely frequent the railways, but all the same . . .

Japan has a climate that is damp and treacherous. Nowhere in the world is there so much lung trouble.

The trees are sickly, puny, meager, rising feebly, growing with difficulty, fighting against adversity, and tortured as soon as possible by man in order to appear still more dwarfish and miserable.

Japanese bamboos: sad, worn-out things, gray and with no chlorophyl; Ceylon would not have them as reeds.

153

Anything that is not mediocre finds no friends here. The cedar must hide behind the sickly cherry tree, the sickly cherry tree behind the plum tree in a pot, the plum tree in a pot behind the thimble-like pine.

The men are ugly, with no sparkle—they are sad, wasted and dry, with the look of petty clerks without a future, of corporals, subordinates, servants of Baron X. and of Mr. Z. or of the papaland* . . . with little pig eyes and decayed teeth.

The women look like servants (always service), the young ones like pretty soubrettes.

They are stocky, short, and above all hefty, and they are all loins from leg to shoulder. The face is sometimes pretty, but the prettiness lacks purpose and emotion; the head is always so big, big with what? with emptiness? why such a big head, for such a small physiognomy and a still smaller expression?

The same in character as in appearance: a great indifferent, insensitive blanket and just a trifle touchy and sentimental (like the military).

Little superficial bursts of laughter like a charwoman, eyes that disappear as though they were sewn up, clothes like a humpback, a fussy way of doing their hair (the geisha's style of hairdressing), achieved by calculations, labor, and symbolism—the whole effect completely silly.

An armor compressing and flattening the breasts with a cushion in the back, painted and powdered one hundred per cent, she embodies the unfortunate and typical creation of this nation of esthetes and sergeants that could leave nothing, no, nothing, to its natural impulse.

Gray houses, with empty, icy rooms, constructed and measured according to a fixed, uncompromising rule.

* In French "papatrie," untranslatable. (Translator's note)

154

Streets like a seaside resort with garlands of little flowers or of little colored lamps. A useless, impermanent look about it. That white, beachlike side of existence.

Identical, expressionless cities resounding with motor-horns. Shrieking like the devil.

A country which, though full to bursting, looks as if it had nothing in it; where neither men nor plants nor houses seem to have any foundation or scope.

An insular mentality, uncommunicative and proud.

A thin and insignificant language, skin-deep, agreeable and pleasant.

A religion of insects, exactly the religion of ants, Shinto-ism (with that famous cult of the ant-hill), an ant people.

A country where everything is known, everything open, everything spied upon, where no door can be closed, where one finds a spy even in one's bath, quite naked, but a spy all the same (they keep you company everywhere); where a young girl who is not very rich is normally sold to a brothel keeper, to serve the multitude (as far as they have individuality!) (service, always service).

A people that is the prisoner of its island, of its masks, of its conventions, of its police, of its discipline, of its wrappings and of the cords that bind it.

But, on the other hand, the most active, the least talkative, the least 'temperamental,' as the English say, the most efficient in the world, the best-tempered, the most self-controlled. Having, without a word, reconstructed Tokyo in ten years; colonized and replanted Korea with trees, industrialized Manchuria. Conquered, modernized, beaten the record, and finally ... what everyone knows.

A people, in fact, devoid of wisdom, of simplicity and of depth, over-serious, though fond of toys and novelties, not easily amused, ambitious, superficial and obviously doomed to our evils and to our civilization.

★

No actor in the world bawls like the Japanese with so little result. He does not speak his part, he mews it, belches it, and he trumpets, brays, neighs and gesticulates like one possessed, and in spite of it all I do not believe him.

All this is done 'on the side,' 'to decorate.' The frightful contortions he makes in the effort to represent his sufferings merely express the hell of a trouble he is taking to express suffering; it is suffering expressed by a man who no longer knows the meaning of it (a lot of esthetes, all of them) in front of an audience of esthetes, equally ignorant of the subject.

He weeps, he moans; a great carcass of groans from which there is nothing to be had.

Like the Japanese smile that only shows the teeth, politeness does not get across.

With voices like old grumblers, trying to give importance to their nonsense, their mediocre language, and their stories of vendettas, with prolonged groans, syllables spun out like she-cats in heat at night in their loneliness and nervous exasperation, Japanese actors are the most false, the most insupportable of all Asia and of Europe (Korean women singers included).

Their drama snarls, with the Voice of the People, the Voice of a Call to Order and of Remonstrance, but completely lacking in grandeur.

A loud voice that reeks of prejudice a thousand miles away, of life taken up by the wrong end, a background of ancient impostures and obligations, and a series of second-rate notions, but spelled with a capital letter, in the midst of which like the voices of the Categorical Imperative (the great master of Japan) the poor characters move about, victims, subordinate creatures, but giving themselves, as one might expect, great swashbuckling airs, with a peculiarly decorative type of courage, and there is such a lack of variety that one sees why in the *No* plays they wear a mask and why at Osaka the actors are simply wooden marionettes, life-size.*

Lest this be mistaken for the conventions of a big theater, go to the small ones, the tiniest ones. Listen to the singers of Yosuri; attend a simple recitation, the same inferno can be found here. First some frigid scenery, very precise, and always well done. Then two women seated facing the audience, one on the right, the other on the left. Two. One reciting or howling, the other accompanying or clucking.

The reciter goes into hysterics seated—she howls, screams, but remains seated. Long periods of a nervous external racket that never touches one, but which at times corresponds more or less to a decorative line of feeling; the other accompanies her on a three-stringed instrument, and with a sort of papercutter taps sharply on the strings, thus producing the sound of sawing. The sawing act comes about every twenty seconds. A despairing sound. The instrument simply gives up the

* *One day I saw an actor who was miming drunkenness. It was quite a while before I realized it. He had made up his part by taking from one drunkard this, from another that, from such a one the break-down of his speech, from another of his gestures, or his fumbling acts, or his lapses of memory; and so with these scraps he had made himself a harlequin's costume for drunkenness that had no connection with any possible drunkard, no center, no truth, and had been constituted as if by a man who did not know what drunkenness was, and would be unable to picture it to his inner self. And yet that seems unbelievable in Japan, which is so full of drunkards. I must say it was amazing.*

157

ghost, and twenty seconds later begins all over again. And so on for twenty-five or thirty minutes. And while she accompanies, she clucks. She goes *'guieng'* (*guieng,* or *rien,* or *nieng*), then silence, then she goes *hom,* with a short, narrow, skipping and ridiculous *o* combining a sniffle, unwillingness, denial, low spirits, and above all a frightful hardness and discipline.

As for Japanese music, even that of the *Geishas,* it is a sort of sour, fizzy water that stings but does not cheer.

It has a false graviy, it tears, with a nervous tearing—the over-shrillness of the horror play. No volume, no poise. It amuses itself pressing and making a martyr of a nerve at the back of the ear.

The whistling of the wind in the reeds, and a certain uneasiness, produce a painful impression of remoteness, but not at all of immensity and of the infinite.

Remember that the motor horn is used in Japan in a useless and intensive manner. This instrument with its sharp notes delights them and makes Tokyo a noisier and more maddening city than Rome or New York.

Modern music: melodies taken from here and there, from gypsies, etc., others peculiar to Japan. Fresh and melodious young girl voices, the kind that are a bit too dovelike.

JAPAN

While many countries that one has liked become, as the distance from them increases, almost ridiculous or insubstantial, Japan, which I distinctly detested, grows almost dear to me.

It is their own fault, too, with their damned police. But there you are, the police do not bother the Japanese, he likes them. He wants order above everything. He does not necessarily want Manchuria, but he wants order and discipline in Manchuria. He does not necessarily want war with Russia and the United States (it is only a consequence), he wants to *clear up* the political horizon.

'Give us Manchuria, let us beat Russia and the United States, and *then* we shall be able to settle down.' I was very much struck by this remark by a Japanese, this desire to *clean up*.

Japan has a mania for cleaning.

In the opinion of a relatively dirty man like myself, washing, like a war, is a trifle puerile, because it has to be done all over again after a while.

But the Japanese likes water, and the *'Samuraï'* likes honor and revenge. The *Samuraï* washes in blood. The Japanese even washes the sky. In a Japanese picture, have you ever seen a dirty sky? and yet!—

He also scrapes the waves clean.

A pure and icy ether reigns over the objects that he draws; as a result of this extraordinary purity, their country is believed to be marvelously bright, whereas it rains there all the time.

Still brighter are their music and their young girls' voices, sharp and piercing, a kind of knitting needle in musical space.

What a far cry from our orchestras with their *tidal waves,* in which that sentimental reveler called the saxophone has recently appeared.

What froze me so at the Japanese theater was the emptiness, which one ends by liking, but which hurts at first and which is authoritarian; and the motionless characters, placed at either extremity of the stage, howling and going off alternatively, at a terribly high pressure, like living *Leyden jars*.

★

I am not one of those who criticize the Japanese for having reconstructed Tokyo in an ultra-modern style, for filling it with cafés, of the Exposition of Decorative Arts type (Tokyo is a hundred times more modern than Paris). For having adopted the precision and purity of geometry in their furnishings and decoration.

One might criticize the Frenchman for being modern, not the Japanese. The Japanese has been modern for ten centuries. Nowhere in Japan do you find the slightest trace of that stupid pretentiousness of what is called Louis XIV, XV, Empire, etc.

To find something beautiful in France, to see a chair that will be fairly satisfactory (as far as a chair may be satisfactory), or a painting, a picture that is honest and plain, one must go back to the fifteenth and sixteenth centuries. When you look at a picture by Clouet (and in fact by Memling, Ghirlandajo, etc.), there is something right, assured, attentive and peaceful in it. Next comes the pompous century, then the century of the boudoir pimp, then the 'stupid nineteenth century,' 'the century of heart trouble.' Since the sixteenth century, the European has been losing himself, and lose himself he must, obviously, so that he may find himself.

In Japan, nothing of the sort; everything was always precise, never over-ornamented (in Japan the houses are not even painted, nor are the rooms, no wallpaper—this kind of pretentiousness is unknown).

The same material for everybody, rich or poor, and one that is never ugly: wood.

No doubt modern geometry is a bit cold. That of Japan was always so. But they have always liked it. . . . Besides, Japan as an imitator seldom goes wrong in the matter of taste. It has not imitated the style of 1900. This idea never occurred to any Japanese. But the ultra-modern style is made for him, or rather, was his own with different materials. In the villages, if a new café is built, it will be completely ultra-modern.

There are something like four thousand ultra-modern cafés in Tokyo, where they serve you with drink and the company of a 'barmaid.' There's no way of being by oneself. No use trying.

★

The European, after many an effort, has succeeded in belittling himself before God.

The Japanese not only belittles himself before God, or before men, but even before the smallest of waves, before the crumpled leaf of the reed, before distant bamboos that he can hardly see. Modesty, no doubt, reaps its reward. For to no other people do the leaves and the flowers appear with so much beauty and fraternity.

KOREA

It must be admitted that European civilization has every fault. But it has a magnetism that sweeps everything else away. There is in the world a general surge toward a joy without depth, toward excitement. The old Japanese music resembles the moaning of the wind; already the new is quite catchy; the old Chinese music is a perfect marvel, sweet and slow; the new sounds like any other; the old Korean music is tragic and terrible, and yet it used to be sung by prostitutes, but now it is 'come along, let's dance.' (Their present music is a vile gallop and expresses in another way those singular transports that are most typical, among all the yellow races, of the Korean); man is no longer the world's prey, but the world is his prey, man is at last emerging from his swamp.

So he *did* suffer with the blues, in the old days, and repression was unbearable to him! Even for an Asiatic.

JAPAN

This happened in the railway station in Okayama (in the stations, on the platforms of incoming trains, there are always quantities of gentlemen, ready to give their combined greetings to important personages on the train).

There are at first five or six hurried salutations on both sides, then it calms down and one can begin to get in a glance between each bow. Presently one may venture to speak, politely, though, of course, with a fresh bow at the first words to remove any doubt as to the good feelings of each one toward the other.

At Okayama, a lady was taking the train. She was there on the platform, in deep mourning, her style of dress exceedingly distinguished (in black, with a few white dots here and there that looked as if they might have fallen by chance, like raindrops).

She stood, during the eight minutes the train stopped, with her back to the compartment, while her waiting-women prepared the places for her, for her son and her brother (though the latter may have been her major-domo) and installed some baskets of flowers, covered with white silk, with one black dot beside the bow.

Thirteen persons in a semi-circle on the platform surrounded her; motionless, no particular sign of any sentiment other than deference. Two or three, however, appeared to be 'touched.' . . .

She meanwhile, very white, blinked her eyelids.

Her eyes were slightly reddened; twice she dabbed them lightly with a little handkerchief hitherto concealed.

She neither looked at anyone in particular nor away in the distance. She was not exactly sad, but was plainly conscious of an important ceremony, and that the actual circumstances in which she found herself were, or should have been, rather 'chic.'

And finally she bent low repeatedly, smiled a little, the train whistle blew a first time, she said three words to her sister(?) when the latter approached, smiled at her distinctly, bowed again to the semi-circle; the semi-circle bowed, bending at right angles; she got on the train, it whistled again and was off.

At that moment one of the group remembered something he wanted to let the major-domo know and ran alongside the train, bowing low as he ran, and bowed and bowed so much that a post in the station, which owing to his bent position he had not been able to see in time, put an end to his race; it must have hurt him considerably.

★

Now that one has spoken of the mentality of certain peoples, one really wonders if it was worth while, if one's time would not have been put to a better use otherwise.

Take as an example a nation supposed to be great, England.

What is the Englishman? Not such an extraordinary creature. But there are fifty-five millions of them. This is the important fact. Suppose you had thirty Englishmen in all, throughout the whole world. Thirty chosen at random. Who would notice them? It is the same way with all the nations. For they are made up of 'the average.'

A nation containing five hundred thousand Edgar Poes would obviously be a little more impressive.

Who will weigh the imbeciles in the scales when a civilization is set up?

★

The yellow soul is the only one that drags no mud along with it. It is never muddy. We do not know what it does with the mud. There is none. I was given, in Singapore, some obscene Chinese postcards. The Chinese has written some obscene things, and among others some plays. Well, what of that? Fifty per cent of the canvases in the Luxembourg seem dirty to me, and yet these obscene postcards seem to me amazingly delicate and quite incapable of causing inner damage. They are not at all exciting. It is not without reason, too, that the Japanese is at home with flowers, worships them and loves them fraternally as others love dogs, and that the Chinese likes to be among the leaves of the willow and of the bamboo.

When I went from Bengal to Darjeeling there was a halt at the Nepalese frontier, and a young Nepalese girl came and smiled at me. I believe she wanted to know whether I would buy some chocolate that she offered to fetch for me from a shop. But she knew no other English word than the one for 'chocolate.' (In a Nepalese there is some Hindu and some Mongol. She was entirely Mongol.) That smile, not in the least awkward, so bright, made such an impression on me and I looked at her with such delight that she herself was moved by it. Finally she broke away as though caught up by the wind, ran to get the chocolates, and put them in my hand. But the car that I was sharing with other travelers was about to leave, there was no hotel, she did not speak English, no one spoke English.

Oh! first smile of the yellow race.

Everything is hard inside me and arid, but that smile of hers, so sweet, seemed to be the mirror of myself.

When I went back, I sought, I looked, I stopped. No one: at last, at the moment when the train whistled and was leaving, someone ran quickly with a light step to my window, breathless, came to smile, to smile for the last time, to smile sadly. So she too remembered. Why did I not go back? Was not my destiny there?

★

A people's dress tells one a great deal more about them than their poetry. Which may come from elsewhere and take everybody in like that of Japan.

Dress is a conception of oneself, worn by oneself.

Who would dream of wearing something that was contrary to himself and that contradicted him constantly?

In adopting a dress, a people sometimes makes a mistake as to what suits it, but rarely. It is not the color of the skin nor the shape of the body alone that guide the choice of clothing, but the soul, the expression. And general concepts.

The Japanese woman is difficult to dress, but there is no necessity for her to compress her breasts as she does, which are fine and well shaped, and to put a cushion on her back: *nothing but a love of discipline.* Japanese dress is extremely decorative, but esthetic.

The Balinese women quite frankly leave the breasts naked.

Mind you, this is not merely by chance; their legs are carefully covered down to the feet with very pretty stuffs that they dye themselves, and they could quite as easily be completely dressed. Besides, nudity *is very difficult to wear;* it is a technique of the soul. It is not enough to remove one's clothing. One must remove one's vileness. (I once saw some nudists in the neighborhood of Vienna. They took themselves for 'nude people.' But all I saw was some meat.)

The poetry of a people is more deceptive than its dress; it is manufactured by esthetes, who are bored and who are only understood among themselves.

Plays are more truthful (at least in the way they are produced), for the public would not go regularly to performances that bored them.

I have seen plays of the Chinese, Koreans, Malayans, Tamils, Bengalis, Hindus, Turks, modern Greeks, Annamites, Hungarians, Spanish, Serbians, etc.; films of the Chinese, Japanese, Bengalis, Hindus, and dances of the Javanese, Balinese, Hindus, Somalis, and of the South American Indians.

The subject is of no importance. Many of them are similar. Likewise, the history of races (everywhere similar) is of little importance. It is the manner, the style and not the facts that matter. A people about which one knows nothing and that has stolen everything from others—ideas, religion, insti-

166

tutions—has its own *gestures,* its *accent,* its *physiognomy* . . .
its *reflexes.*

And each man has a face that betrays him, and his face,
at the same time, betrays his race, his family and his religion.
Everyone is responsible for his face.

No one wears it undeservedly.

Will there be another war? Look at yourselves, Europeans, look at yourselves.

Nothing is peaceful in your faces.

All is struggle, desire, avidity.

Even peace you want violently.

A BARBARIAN
WITH THE MALAYS

Malays, Javanese of Sumatra, Balinese, Malay Sundanese of Borneo, of Flores, mixed with, married to a hundred insular races, to the Bataka, to the Dyaks, to the Chinese, to the Arabs, and even to the Papus, converted in turn to the religion of India (Hinduism and Buddhism), then to Mohammedanism —here is enough to trip up anyone who attempts to generalize at every step. It is annoying.

THE BARBARIAN IN MALAYA

The Malay has something wholesome, noble, clean and human about him.

The Chinese, the Hindu, all those original races compare unfavorably with him. Besides, originality is a defect, the outward sign of defects.

He is precise, neat. Many of them remind one of the Basques.

171

Unfortunately, I shall hardly get to know the Malays. . . . There is not a thing I do not like about them. Not a form. Not a color. Their houses, their trains, their boats, their hotels and their clothes, everything pleases me. They have the same taste as mine for oblique forms (straight towers are pretentious looking and at the same time rather silly).

The houses, with their concave roofs, look like waves, their boats look as if they were sailing along the sky. The comma is the keynote of everything.

The Malay *kriss,* the only really beautiful weapon, nonchalant like its master, but also firm, easy to hold, and looking for trouble, seems made for blows at random on the body of a crowd.

The Malay hates an outburst. When he gets angry, it is really because he cannot bear things any longer, he is out of patience. Then his anger makes havoc and ends by his own death.

The Malays are the only people whose constructions please me. It would disgust me to own a house. Making an exception, at Johore, I inquired the cost of buying a house: two hundred francs. The whole effect modest, but pleasant; on piles, three rooms, some corridors, a penthouse, all in wood so light that it cannot weigh more than three hundred kilos.

Batik, the only dress material that does not hurt one's eyes, that does not snatch one's attention.

Therefore, the Malay, who is lazy like a well-bred man, has, even if he is poor, a charming house, though with nothing pretty about it.

In Malaya there are no ugly houses for the common people.

If you see an ugly one, a European or a Chinaman lives in it.

172

The Malay is kind, open-armed, full of humor, a great mocker.

In their plays, where combined decorative and stylized movements abound, they often throw in one or two odd pauses while they busy themselves doing a mime without words, extremely soberly, as though it were not intended for the public, and this is quite comical.

The behavior of the Javanese is so sympathetic, while that of the Balinese I found distinctly less so when I perceived that they are particularly anxious to be proper. The Malay likes propriety.

Batik is very proper. This had never occurred to me. Their style of hairdressing even more so.

The Balinese woman is dressed in a mere trifle, but this trifle, dark-colored (violet-brown) is completely proper in design.

Neither sober, nor pure, nor eloquent, but proper.

They all have deportment. Malays, Javanese, Balinese; their deportment does not suggest excessive dignity or pride, nor is it transcendental. It is deportment.

A Javanese dancer never seems ridiculous, exaggerated or naïve, as those elsewhere are so apt to be, for the thing that most resembles the dance is grandiloquence.

A Javanese dress material can be offered to anyone, to no matter whom, anywhere in the world; it is always 'in good taste.'

The Balinese women leave their breasts bare. They are not all completely unapproachable. Nevertheless, if something has displeased them, it is not sorrow, nor anger, nor sulking that reveals the fact, but an offended look, the look that one knows so well, that belongs only to proper people; and if she does something wrong, she immediately has the impression not of wrong but of impropriety, and I could tell a personal anecdote about this the main theme of which makes me laugh heartily every time I think about it.

Nothing about the Malay is offensive. His face does not reveal abnormal appetites, vices, or defects in his character.

The Malay forgets many things. He forgets everything that is said to him. He will never forget to walk properly. He is proper to the depths of his soul. And the Javanese even more so.

The Javanese without his little scarf properly arranged on his head would not dare to go out.

And when he goes out, he swings his arms a great deal, dangling them. You will not see him playing the fool. No indeed.

*

The Javanese has something about him that does not go forward, but backward.

The Javanese face seems as though it had been wrought like the pebbles in torrents, polished by continual rubbing.

His face has suffered a setback.

Not only is his forehead rounded, but an eternal hand seems to be placed on him, pressing him down and holding back his personality.

Foreheads that do not fight, foreheads that escape and all they ask is to turn back.

His face is hollow like a saucer, not bellicose but submissive; the nose is turned up, yet wide and flat at the end; the head of an orang-outang, and often the head of a frog.

The face of the Javanese woman is marvelously obedient, restful, almost musical.

All Malayan things express a particular fondness for the

cockspur form, almost an obsession with them (and joined to the stiff, upright prow, but a prow placed behind).

The cockspur is one of the few natural weapons in the animal world that is turned in a backward direction.

The hilt of the kriss is in this well-known shape.

The roofs of the houses of the Minangkabau, in Sumatra, resemble waves fastened down. The wave starts, dashes on, there it is at its maximum, at its crest. It is going to break at the point where the roof ends. The roofs rolling away are a magnificent sight; they have as many as twenty crests.

The Javanese hat has two oblique points.

The Javanese actor is one of the few people in the world who wears his chief ornament in the back.

And this pointed ornament that he has on his shoulders, a sort of prow (no stern), a singular thrusting-out from the shoulders, rather makes one think of the exaggerated animation of the wagtail's behind.

Balinese actors almost always turn their backs to each other; even if it is a prince courting a princess, progress is parallel, they never turn round.

The Javanese and the Balinese go along the road in single file (even where there is no danger whatever from traffic), talk to each other without moving their heads; nor will anybody who calls out to them in passing make them do so. If hailed, they always manage to avoid turning round, so odious would this lack of deportment appear to them.

They sit with faces turned toward their houses, their backs to the road, as if they had an eye in their shoulders. In many cases, indeed, in their shoulders, something is there that we lack.

In their music the pentatonic scale is used, the flat scale, the scale that does not get stuck.

175

Nowhere in the world is there music less catchy than the Balinese and Javanese *gamelan*. The *gamelan* utilizes only percussion instruments. Gongs, muffled drums (the tredang), metal kettles (trompong), metal disks (the gender).

Never do these instruments tell or take hold. But they are not so much percussion instruments as instruments of emerging sound; the sound emerges, a round sound that comes to pay a visit, floats around, then disappears. The resonance is stopped by the fingers, feeling their way, seriously, attentively, in the great carcass of sound.

Even the dancers who tell of the love of a prince and a princess tell nothing at all. This is the prince, this is the princess. And they push each other away instead of coming together.

The Balinese dance is a dance with the hand held flat, a dance with the palms open. It neither gives nor rejects, it gropes along the invisible walls of the atmosphere. It is spread out and blind.

The pupils seek the corner of the eye, go to the extreme end, change place in a lateral movement. The neck is dislocated laterally, nothing goes forward; everything aspires to the horizontal, to the immense, to the mural, to a sort of immense *façade,* for everything moves in a space that is absolute and mural. Most of the time the dancers are held by their knees to the ground, tortured there on the spot (by degrees, impatient movements on the spot, shudders like the ripples on a lake, hypnotism, delirium without frenzy, a sort of petrification, of stratification, of the inner self). A music that covers, that covers one in darkness, and in which one finds rest and support.

And who is responsible for this music? Men? No, in Bali,

176

all that resounds, plays, lives, terrorizes, vibrates, comes from 'the demons.'*

BALI

The Dutch are perfectly delighted to possess an island where the women's breasts are bare.** So once and for all they have forbidden the entrance of the island to missionaries, who would promptly have had the breasts hidden, destroying at the same time any interest the place might have had for the tourist. If a missionary does come, it has to be secretly, in the strictest incognito and with false passports, like a Russian Communist.

Are we so much in need of demons? When one arrives in Bali, from Koeboetambakan on, one is enchanted. There are demons everywhere, at the entrance of temples, of houses.

Men, animals, plants—no, decidedly that does not make a world; one must have demons. Carving a demon means adding something to the population of the island. But to carve women and men, what is the use? Just as if one did not know them, as if one had never seen such a thing. . . .

* *The finest theatrical performance that I saw was at a Malay theater in Singapore. Fishermen armed with knives and faggots of reeds fought against a kind of saw-fish. The struggle was formidable. Yet so unbelievably stressed, that the infinitely diverse movements seemed woven in some mechanism and to belong to another world.*

** *The Balinese women go bare-breasted. Already the Javanese women's dress is exceedingly low-cut, leaving as much of the breasts exposed as possible, stopping just at the nipple, entirely uncovering the place where the breast is separated into two hemispheres, that hollow which disturbs schoolboys so much.*

And in the Javanese countryside, a woman with her breast quite naked is not an unheard-of sight.

Besides, their demons in Bali are not irritating and idiotic like those of Southern India, they are quite orderly and they hold a club in their hand, look more as if they were bluffing than really terrible; are not at all frightening, and take part, in spite of their grimaces, in a certain gaiety such as may be found in a pleasant tropical island. The Balinese people live with the demons. There is one at the door of every house. They could not do without it; it is their presence that makes a cremation so interesting. But I am not acquainted with the symbolism of the ceremony.

Some of them (represented by Balinese) catch hold of the coffin, the shroud, with a few bamboos around it; there are forty-odd of them and the struggle begins. The object of certain ones is to reach a platform where the corpse, when it gets there, will enjoy about half an hour's quiet. (The object of the others is to prevent this.) But now the struggle is at its height, a scrimmage in which the coffin gets lost while at the same time the fighters' heads go down, plunge as in football —scrimmage from which a drowned man's head emerges from time to time, a head overcome by a pathetic and rather decorative fatigue, nearly a faint; out of which also arise suddenly proud faces! 'Oh! no, you shan't have it. No indeed. Just come and see . . .' curt challenges follow, a certain lack of actual rage. Thereupon the steps leading to the platform are approached. Ha! none of that. It is too soon!

And the priest throws water on their shoulders.

Immediately the demons begin to wake up. We shall see what we see. And in fact, the scuffle is getting farther away from the platform.

After a quarter of an hour of renewed fighting and fresh buckets of water, the group is clinging to the bottom of the steps. Once more for and against. The people on the steps and on the platform show they are determined to repel every attack. Nothing, as far as one can see, has been gained, when all of a sudden, in one second, the coffin is passed like a cigar. It is there on the platform. But alone.

The demons have been pushed back. One has fainted. A half-dozen are stretched out, their backs on the grass, unable henceforth to aid a dead man to go in one direction or another. However, after a half-hour's rest, the corpse, escorted anew, must again be delivered up to the assault of the demons, and transported to the place of cremation.

However, at the supreme moment of the incineration, nine-tenths of the people have left.

★

Balinese women have more breast than expression. After a time at Bali, one ends by looking at the men.

The European who sees bare breasts cannot help thinking that something is going to happen. But nothing does happen. So he gets accustomed to it.

I am deeply convinced that I would accustom myself very rapidly to seeing these women completely nude.

A breast hardly expresses anything. It is the face that one consults to know the kind of character one is dealing with. The women, in fact, among themselves look each other in the eye, but they do not look at each other's body.

The breasts of the Balinese women are beautiful, well, that is all. And very much in harmony with their pleasant, not very expressive faces.

I remember having been struck and disillusioned many a time in France by the fact that a woman's breasts, when I happened to see them uncovered, were only beautiful, while

179

the face was so wrought by intelligence, by a soul so odd and so exceptional, that I had been persuaded somehow that the breasts too would be exceptional and original. But a breast is not a face.

Although I know these things very well, nevertheless every time I saw the breasts of an intelligent woman they bestialized and transformed her for me so much, so much. Young girls with such touching expressions became, though they did not themselves suspect it perhaps, good for nothing but to be enjoyed by and to belong to everybody.

One of the things one is most struck by in Bali is the women who have ceased to be women. They have got over it. In some cases where the breasts had been too distended they were shriveled up and lay almost flat on the chest, which was now shaped like that of a man.

The face had reverted long ago to the male type and had lost all trace of femininity. The Malayan bones are visible. The woman is not frail, but she is transitory. In some cases she retains but few traces of the feminine character, like souvenirs of a journey. The woman makes the man. She makes a few of them. Then goes to pieces.

★

What the Americans like so much about the Balinese is that 'they *are friendly,*' a thing that is very much appreciated and that one finds among Americans also.

The Balinese like festivals; not a day is without one. There are plays and dancing. And where there is one going on, everybody comes in, everybody is invited, relatives, friends, strangers, foreigners.

One evening, I was late setting about it, I arranged for a

performance of *Wayang Koelit* to be given at the house of a native. When I got there we were absolutely alone, the orchestra, my three guests and myself.

Two hours later, we were lost in a crowd of six hundred persons. The smell of Malayan bodies surrounded us like smoke, vendors of cakes had installed themselves at the door. Laughter came from all sides at the proper time, one had difficulty getting out, and then (we left before the end) many people were still coming in.

★

The Malayan, like the Japanese, has nothing of the transcendental, no philosophy—other people's religion (but only as an ornament), and a certain taste.

The resemblance between the Malayan and the Japanese (mind you, it is the Japanese who is the probable borrower, if borrowing there has been, and not merely a relationship between races) that struck me the most, was at the shadow-theater in Bali.

The puppets do not particularly resemble the puppets of Osaka (though the Malay like the Japanese is 'proper'). (What Japanese would go without an umbrella?) But it was the shrieking, horror-play voice of the Japanese actor, the same behavior, the same voice production, the same manner of expression, though in Balinese, a tongue that is quite remote from the Japanese. And this accompanies every manifestation of Japanese and Balinese art. (But the Balinese actor is naturally not so unpleasant.)

★

The *Wayang Koelit* (shadow-play) of Java is really the same as the *Wayang Koelit* of Bali, but the style is quite different.

The Balinese is still close to the demons.

His music is full of impatience, of trembling, of fever.

It is satanic. The marionettes (cut out of leather) fight each other with unheard-of violence, fast and excitedly. The actor shrieks. The light flickers constantly, making the characters tremble on the screen with a strange life, palpitating, trepidating and electric.

Once the light is cast on the screen it passes through the perforations, outlines and at the same time illuminates them with the clearness of evidence or of stern reality, or rather of a super reality sliced with a knife and taken out of the sky.

Then, when their act is ended, they withdraw, blurred and at the same time vibrating (the actor's hand shakes them constantly), coming back soon afterward, sudden and refulgent on the canvas, giving a tremendous impression of magical petrifaction and of violence that no film could convey.

In the *Wayang Koelit,* the light is motionless. The characters, most of the time, are stuck by their base in the stump of a bamboo that is parallel with the stage. They move the arms rather than the body, arms that are limp and dangling. Even their fighting is not terribly fierce. But the action being accompanied by a continuous noise like pistol shots, the inner tension is achieved.

Their voices (the voices of those reciting) are soft, melodious, low and reflective, and as though merciful; the words, polite, deeply felt, ornate, dreamy voices, almost absent, church voices, a singing that often recalls the Bengali songs, their meditative songs.

The Bengali language is too contemplative. (It can only

182

say â, â, â, ô; the other vowels are always treated like poor relations). The Javanese language is full of meaning, of the meaning of life, grave, good and lazy.

Who has not been moved by the *Tabe Touan,* in Bali (Good day, Sir) said so sweetly; by their way of saying *orang* —not in the French manner, to be sure, stumbling along, *ou, au,* like scaring away the wolves, but a light and quite lively *a,* and the *u,* that surrounds it like a pond, and a gentle good *g,* that picks up and tucks in, and carries away the whole thing, a whole thing quite lively like an eel? *Wayang orang.*

Now the Chinese language is good, but it is dull and washed-out.

A friend said to me at a dance performance in Bali: They look like hens in a hen-coop.

It is quite true. Like hens in a hen-coop; the neck is all that works.

In the modern Bali plays, rows of squatting men, playing sparrows on a branch, in rows of eight or nine, dislocating their necks, rolling their eyes and grumbling but not flying away, and aside from that, bluffing it out as much as to say: 'Hold onto me, fellows, back there. Or I might make trouble.'

★

What I was able to see of the Malayan theater of the present day in Singapore (one of them was called the *Grand Opera of Borneo*) was not unpleasant, but it did not amount to much. Dancers with horrible short dresses, oscillating from one leg to the other, in one spot, glued by who knows what 'chewing

183

gum,' tunes that were slow, sentimental, muddy, variety-show, themes for a primary school; masters and servants, nobleman and prince, mother and son, self-sacrifice, the great dramatic scene, entreaty, getting down on one's knees, great operatic airs, headdress of warriors or rather of noblemen, a kind of Egyptian eureus forty centimeters high; idiotic effects, the fondness for great ceremonies, raised seats, bowing down, and also gross farces right in the middle of the show, kicks on the bottoms of minor characters, bad jokes and something that smelled all over the place of the scourge of the sentimental.

★

Someone who knew fish only through the aquarium of Batavia would have a singular notion of them, but on the whole rather correct. He would know that neither the color, nor the shapes, nor the aspect are what characterize a fish. A toothbrush, a cab, a rabbit may be a fish; it all depends on the insides.

I saw a young example (old ones are quite different) of *Ostracium cornutum,* which is nothing but a little calf's head. This head navigates. A block with a tiny mustache that vibrates. One must look closely to perceive it. Is that all? Not absolutely. This head has a tail, not a body, but a tail; cut a match in two, well, half of the match, but suppose it to be rather flexible, and there it is.

★

Take it all in all, it is possible that the colonials may have done less harm to the colonies than they seemed fated to do.

Look at a little Dutch boy. It is an inharmonious creature,

184

apt to shout, roar, break, destroy, and to assert the weight of his dangerous imagination.

As an adult, the Dutchman will be considerably more phlegmatic. But perhaps he may destroy and alter more coldly, more scientifically the things around him.

★

There are everywhere such invasions of different races, Huns, Tartars, Mongolians, Normans, etc., and such an afflux of religions, Islamic, Buddhistic, Animist, Nestorian, Christian, etc., that no one is pure; each one is composed of a horrid mixture, not counting the prejudices that he has acquired in his own country.

Therefore, when one retires into oneself, flees from the world, and when one succeeds in getting rid of that enormous superstructure and that multiple controversy, one attains to a peace, on a plane so unheard of that one might ask oneself if this is not the 'supernatural.'

★

What is a civilization? A blind alley.

No, Confucius is not great.

No, Tsi Hoang Ti is not great, nor Gautama Buddha, but since then nothing better has been done.

A people should be ashamed to have a history.

And the European just as much as the Asiatic, naturally.

It is in the future that they must see their history.

POSTSCRIPT

And now, said Buddha to his disciples, when about to die:
    'In the future, be your own light, your own refuge.
    'Seek not another refuge.
    'Go not to seek refuge other than in Yourselves.'

    'Pay no attention to another's way of thinking.
    'Hold fast in your own island.
    'GLUED TO CONTEMPLATION.'